AF487824

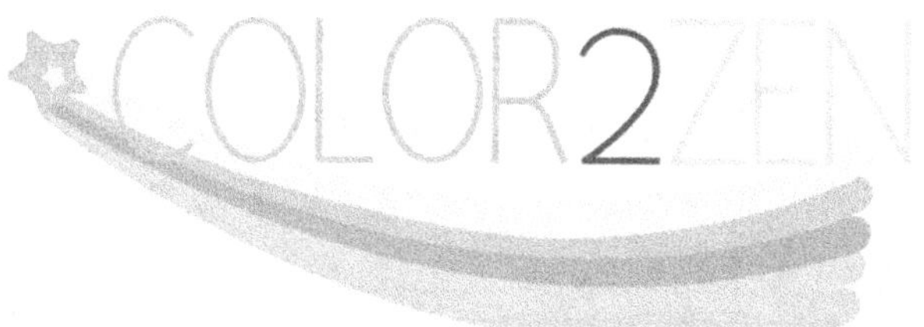
COLOR2ZEN

This book belong to

____

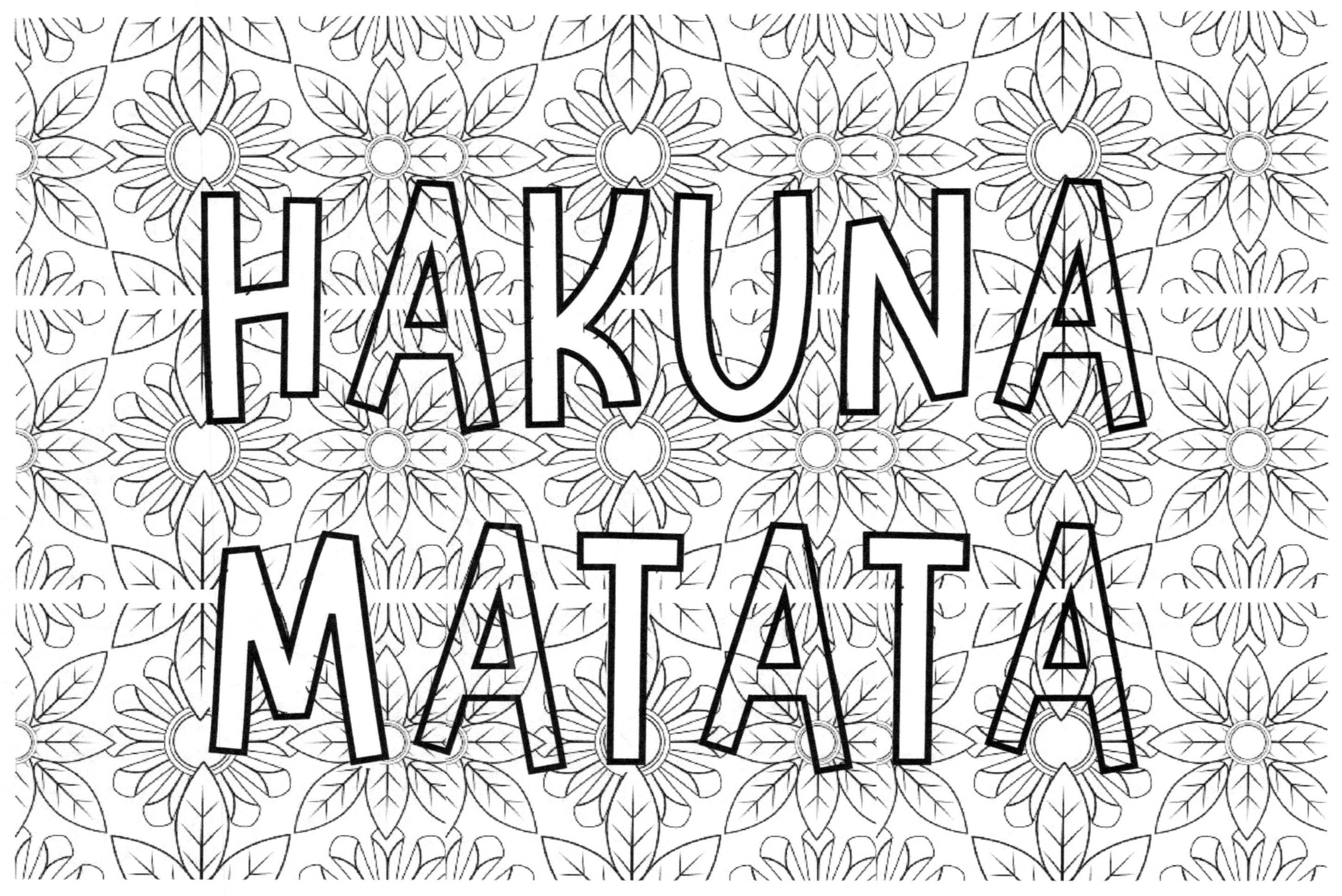

HAKUNA
MATATA

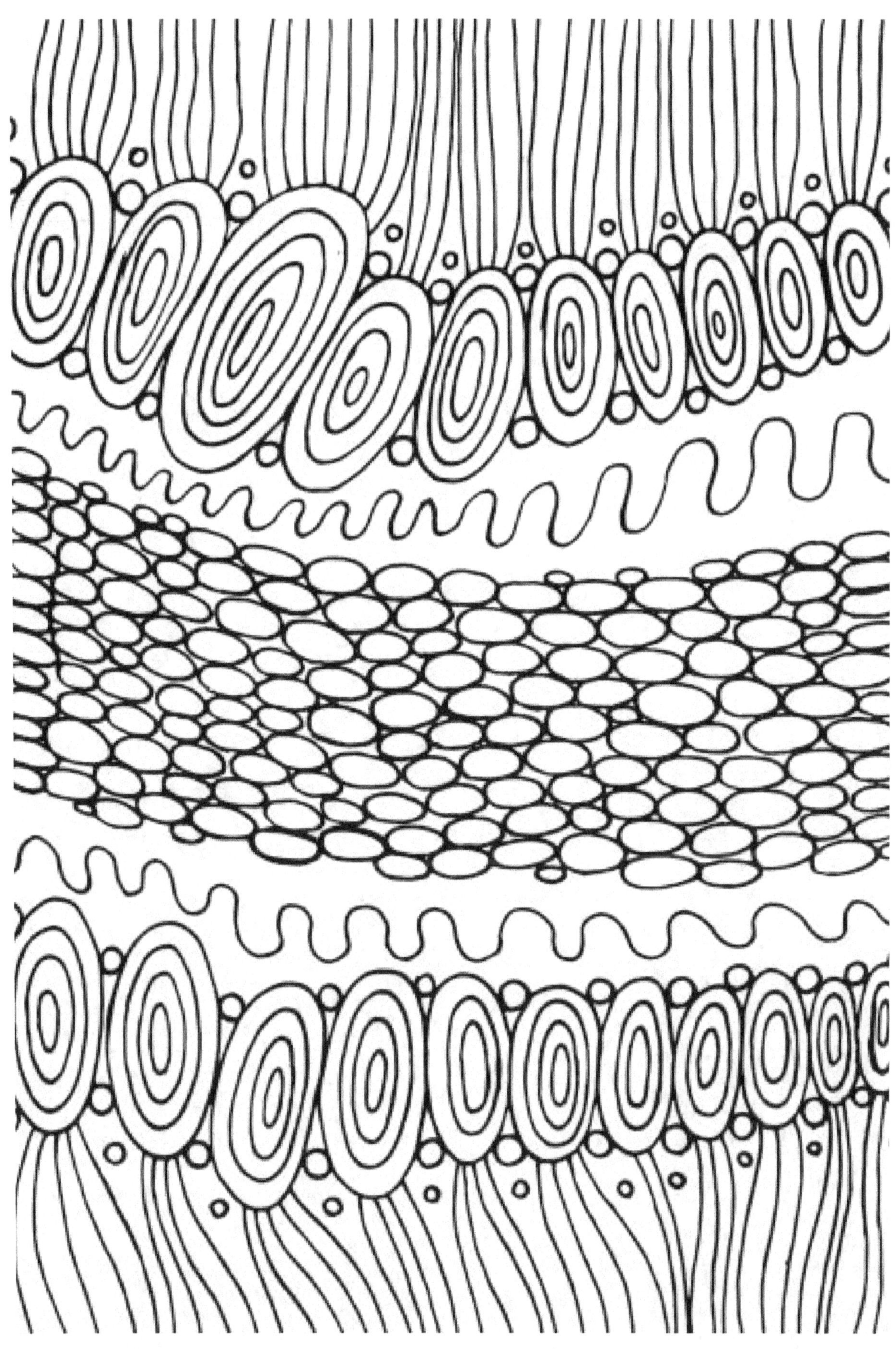

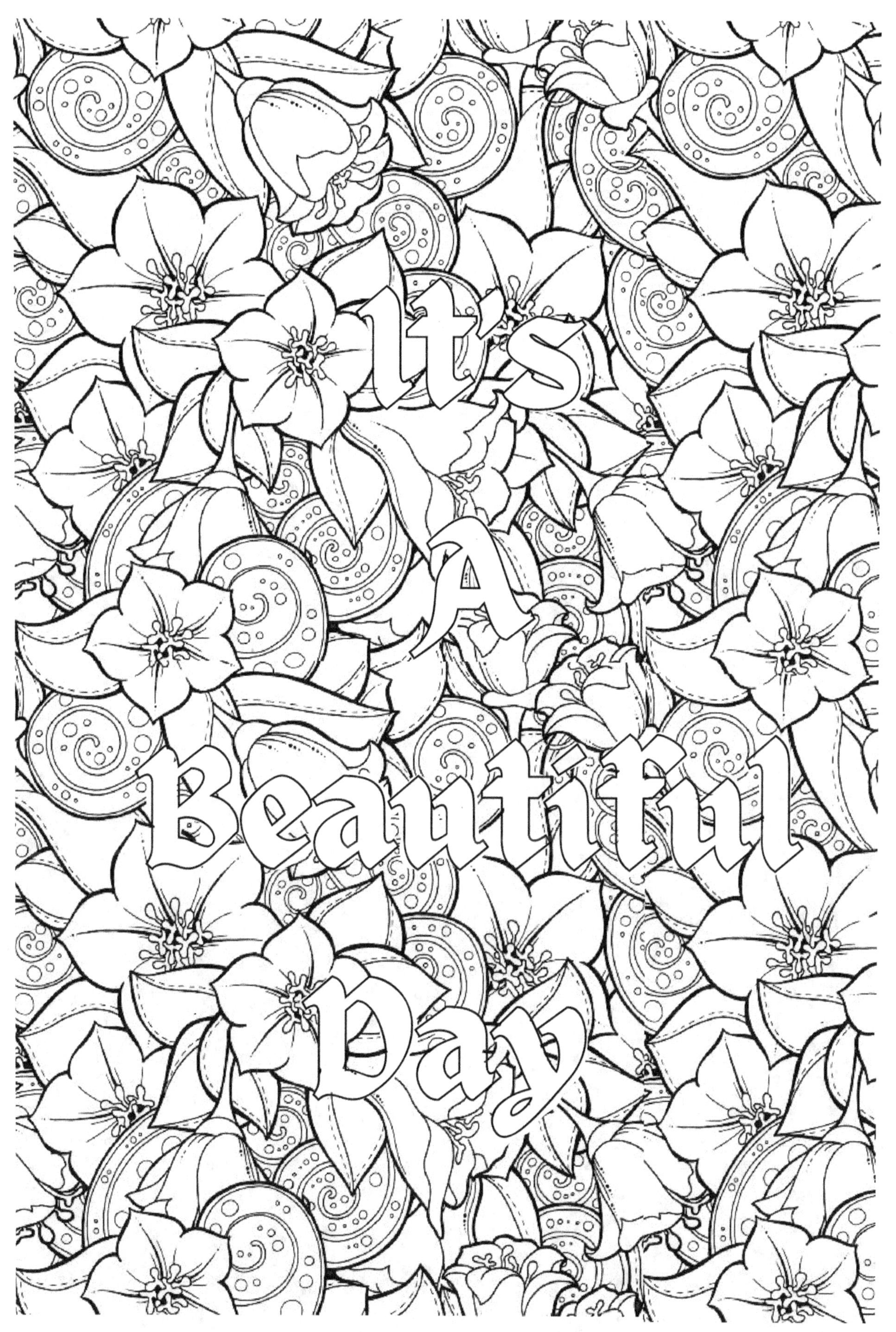
It's
A
Beautiful
Day

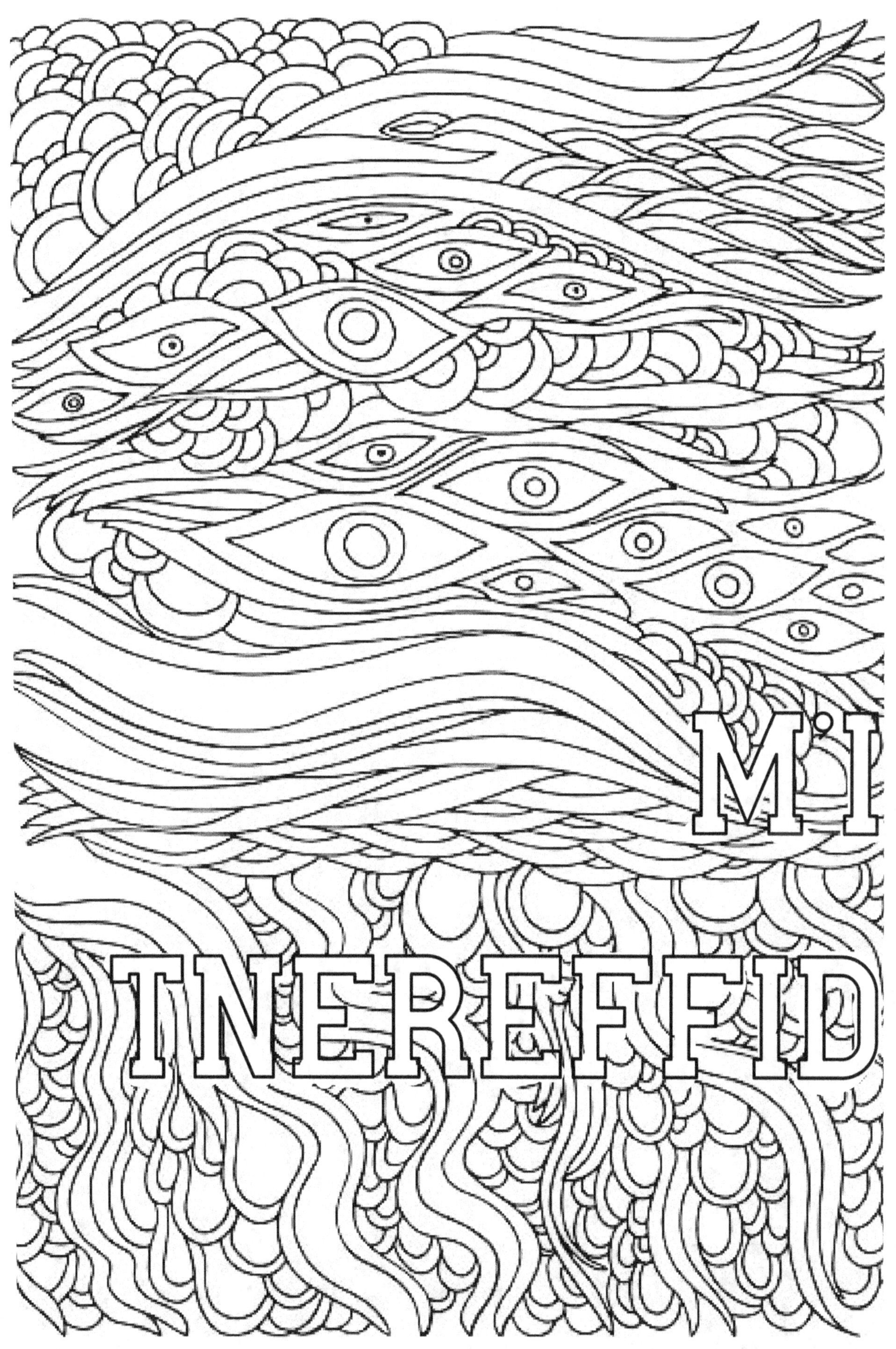
M'I
TNEREFFID

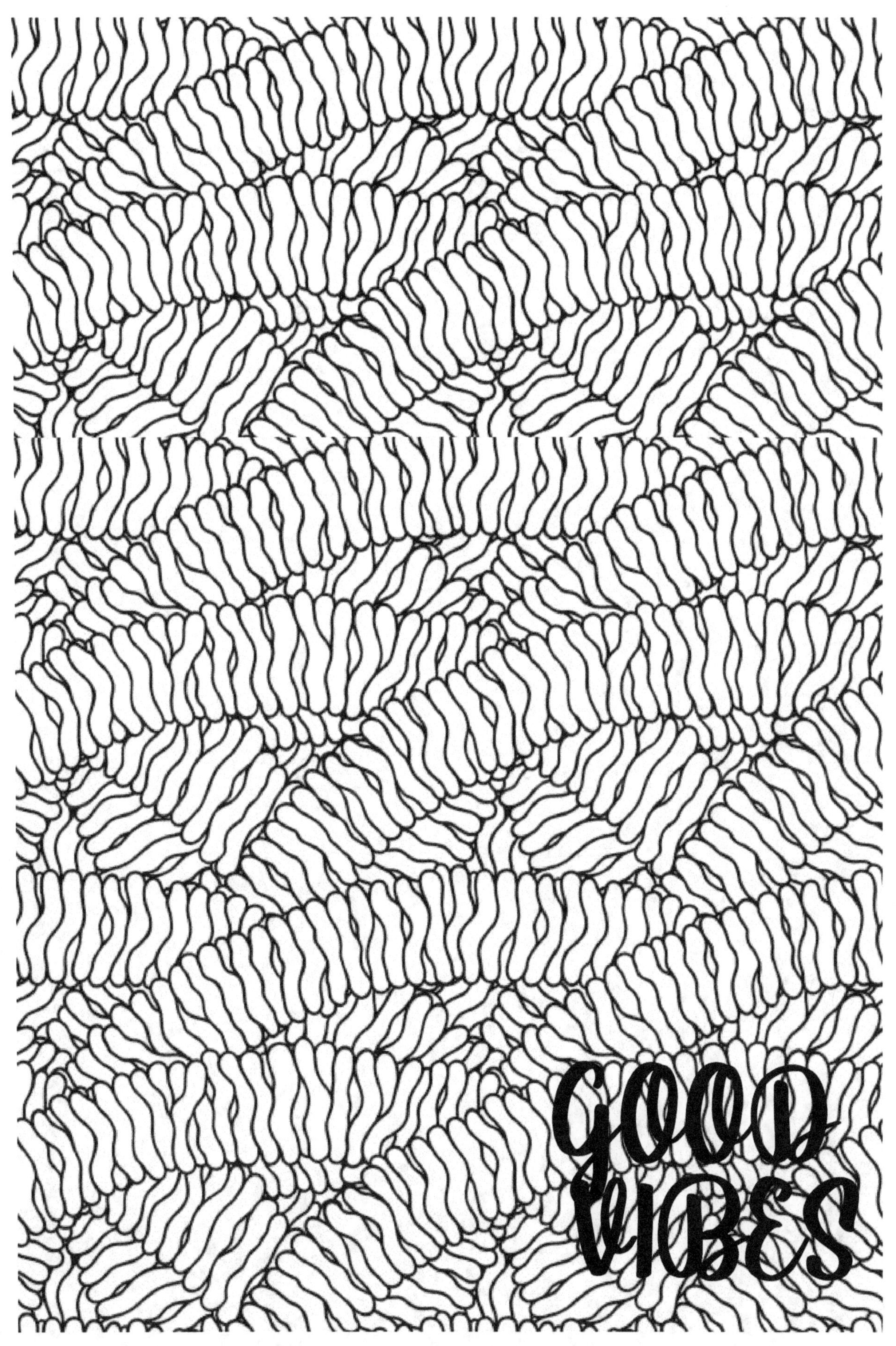

good
vibes

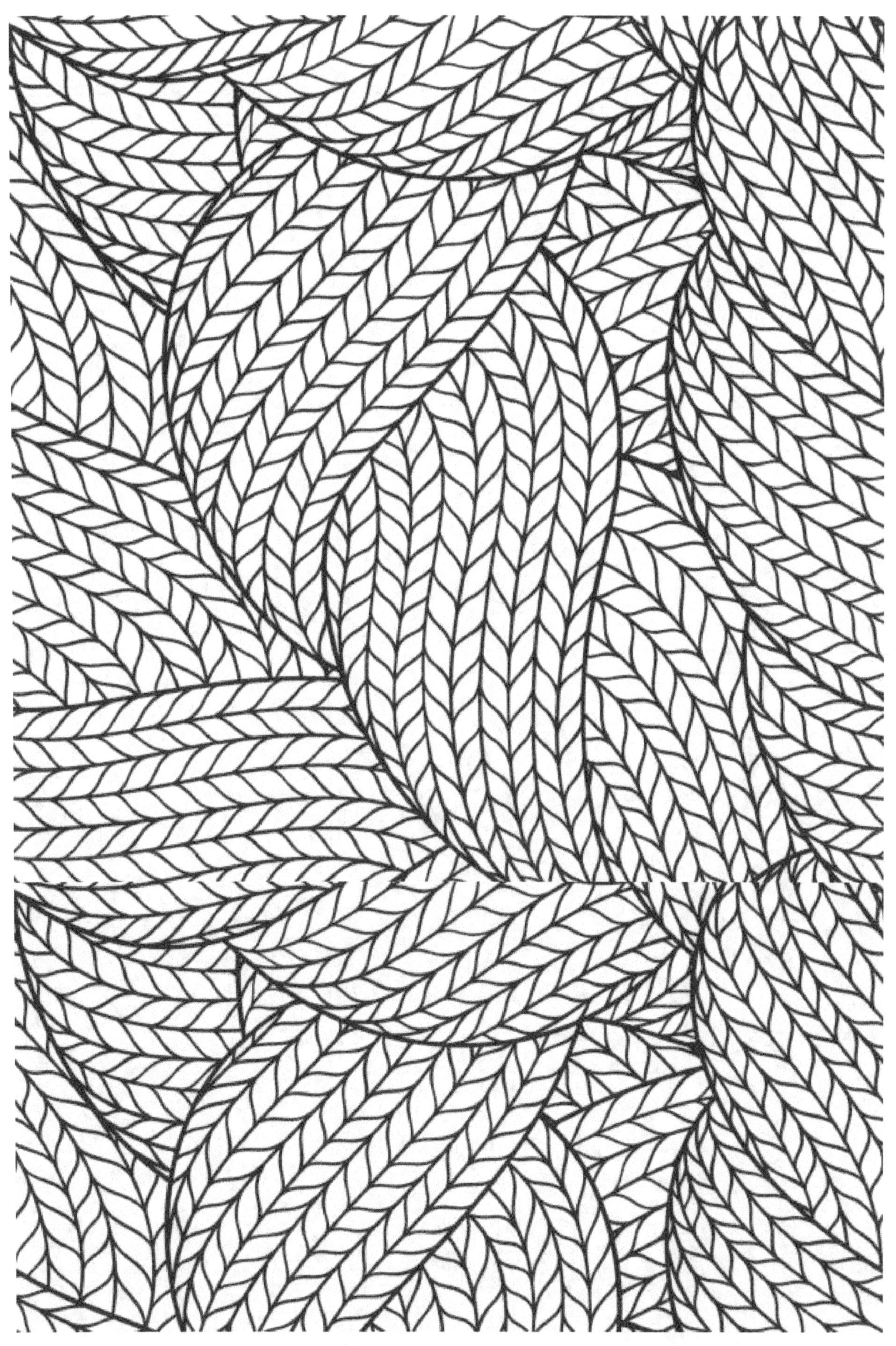

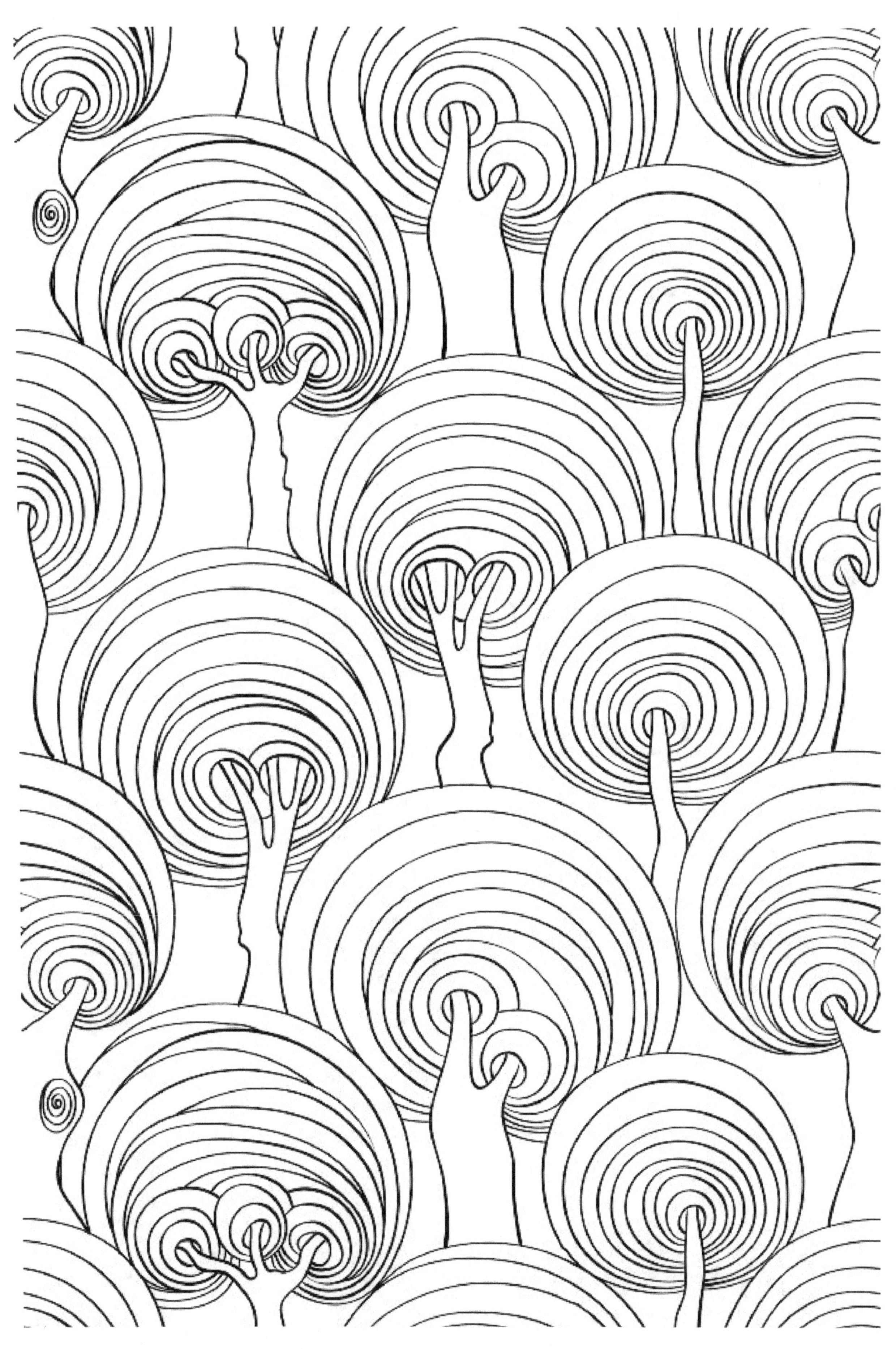

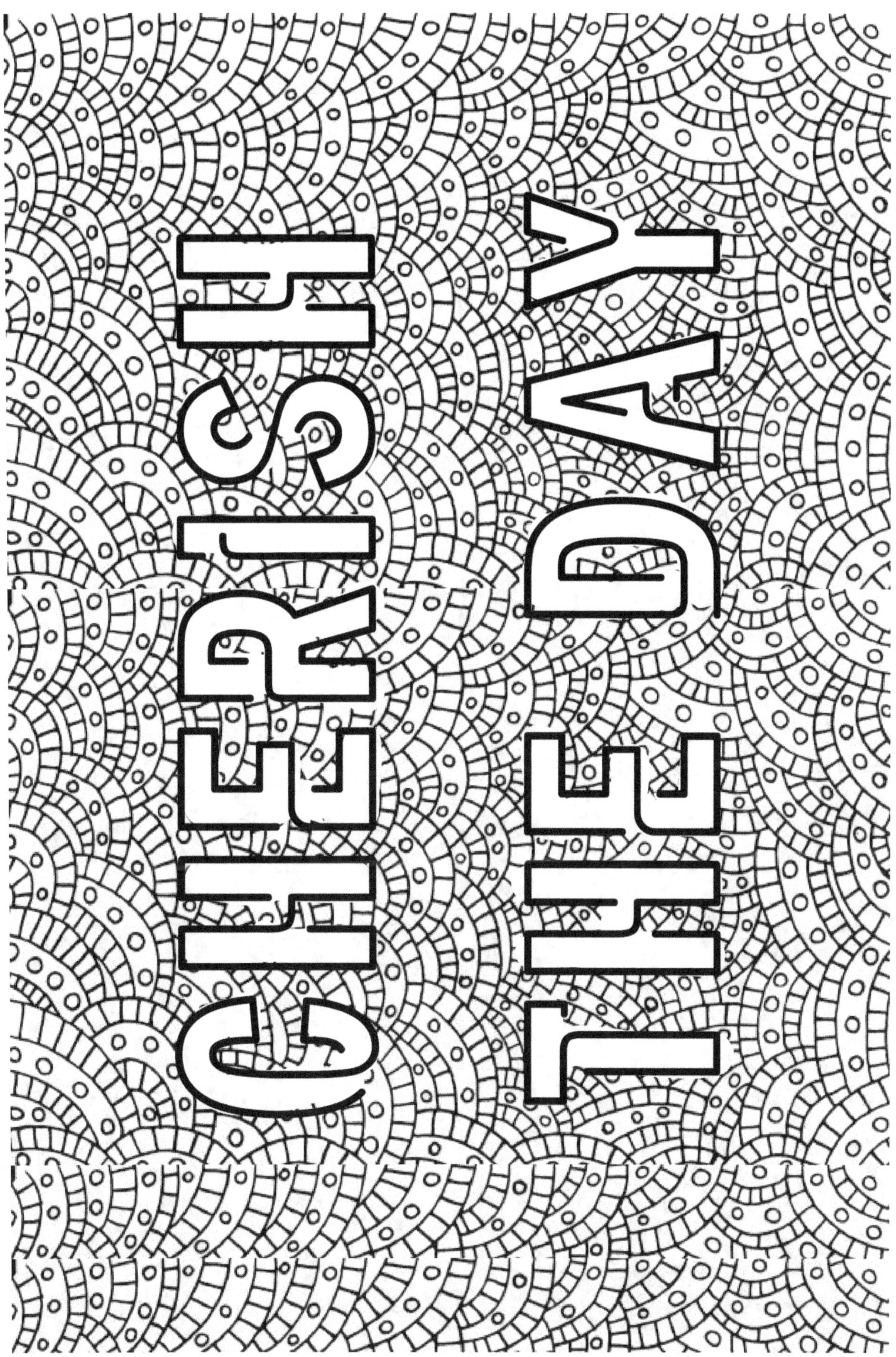

CHERISH
THE DAY

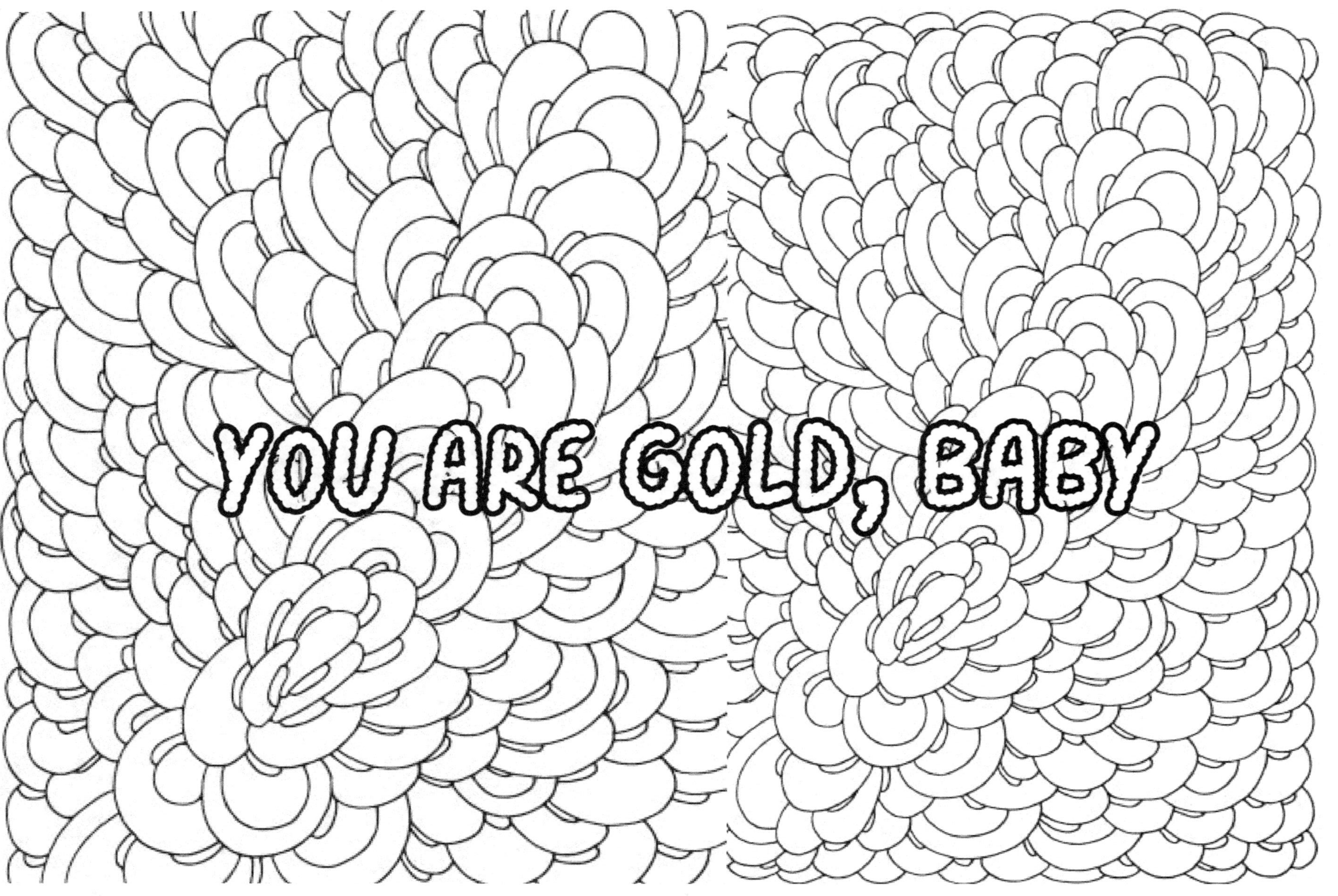

YOU ARE GOLD, BABY

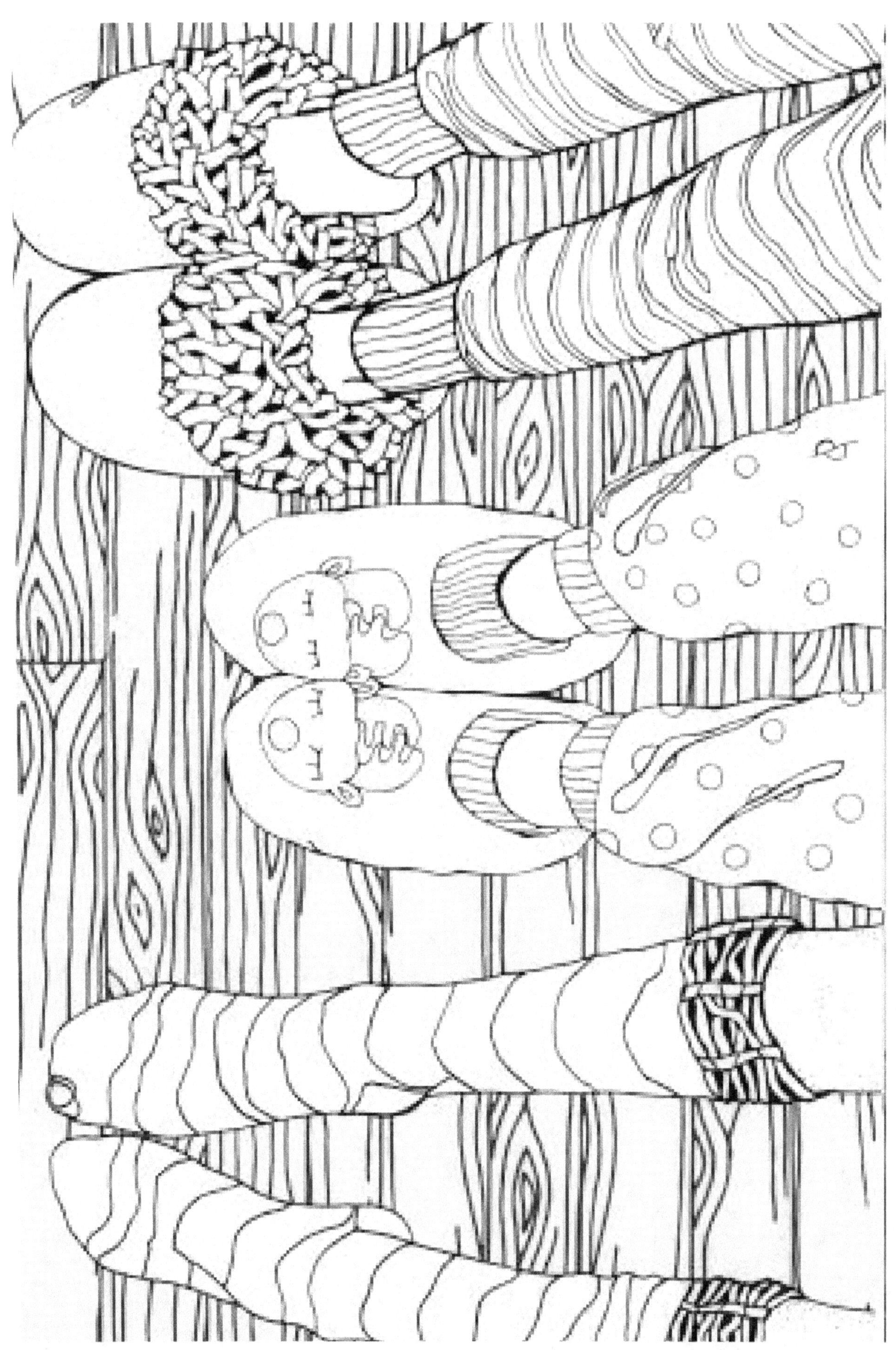

BURN
IT
DOWN

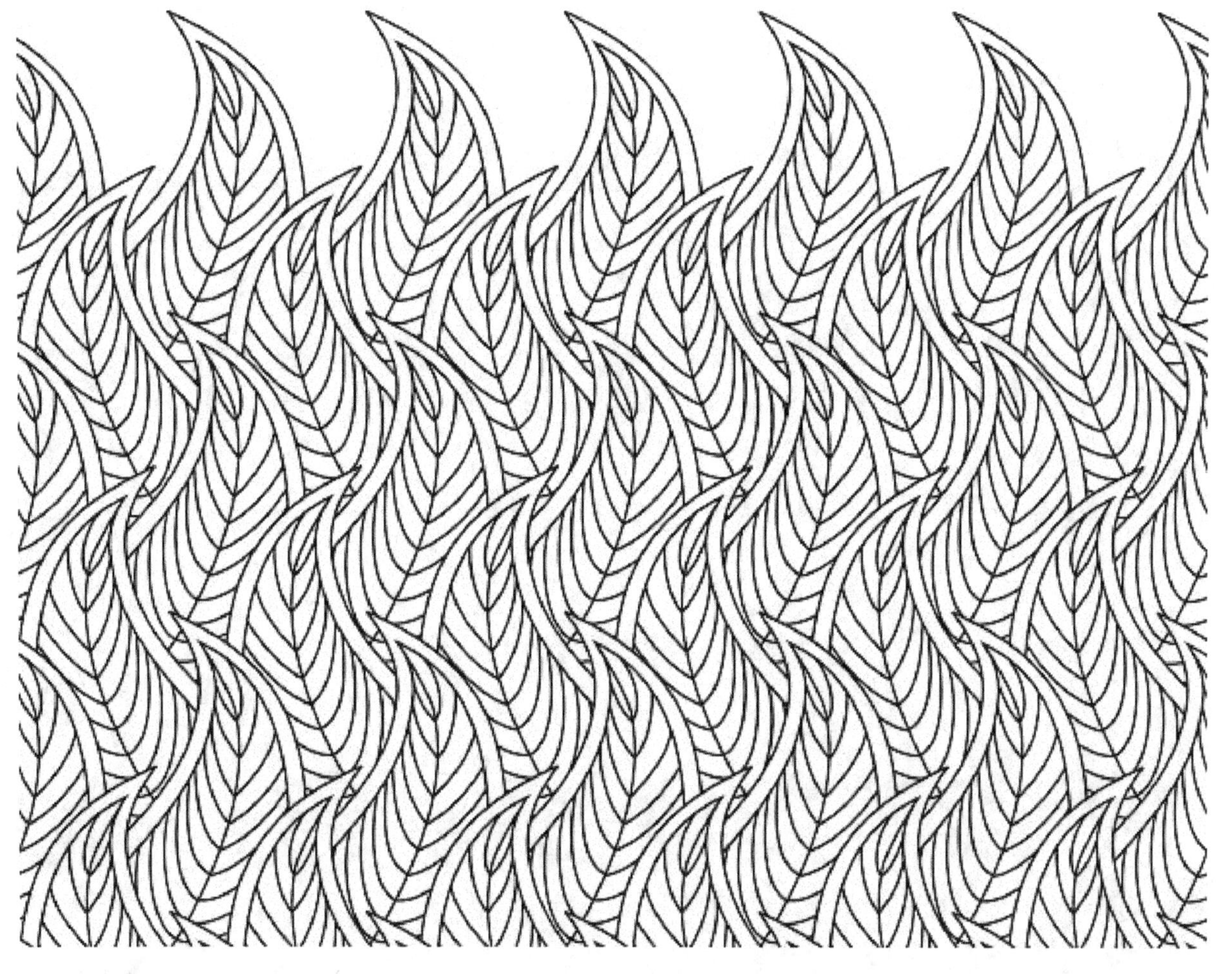

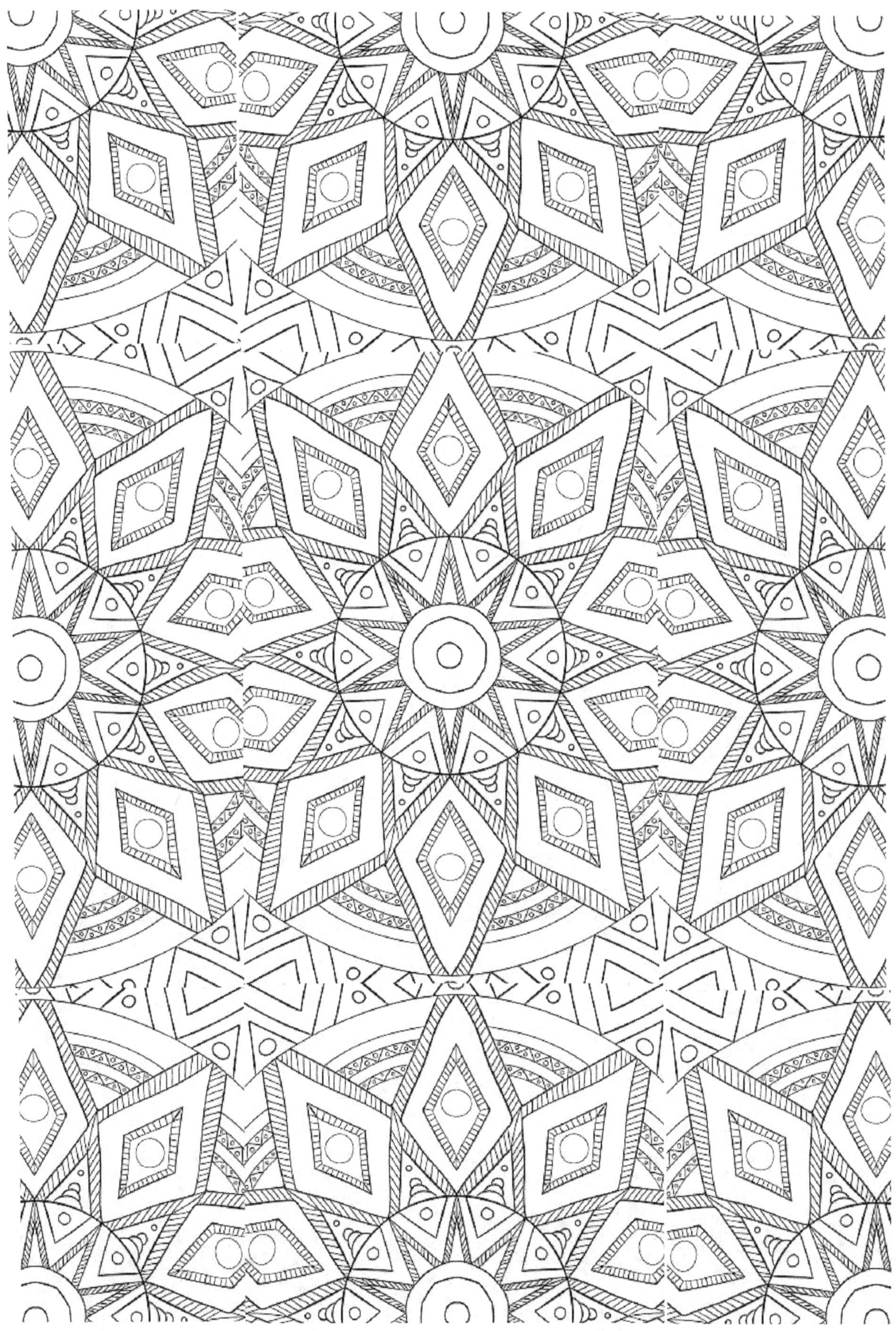

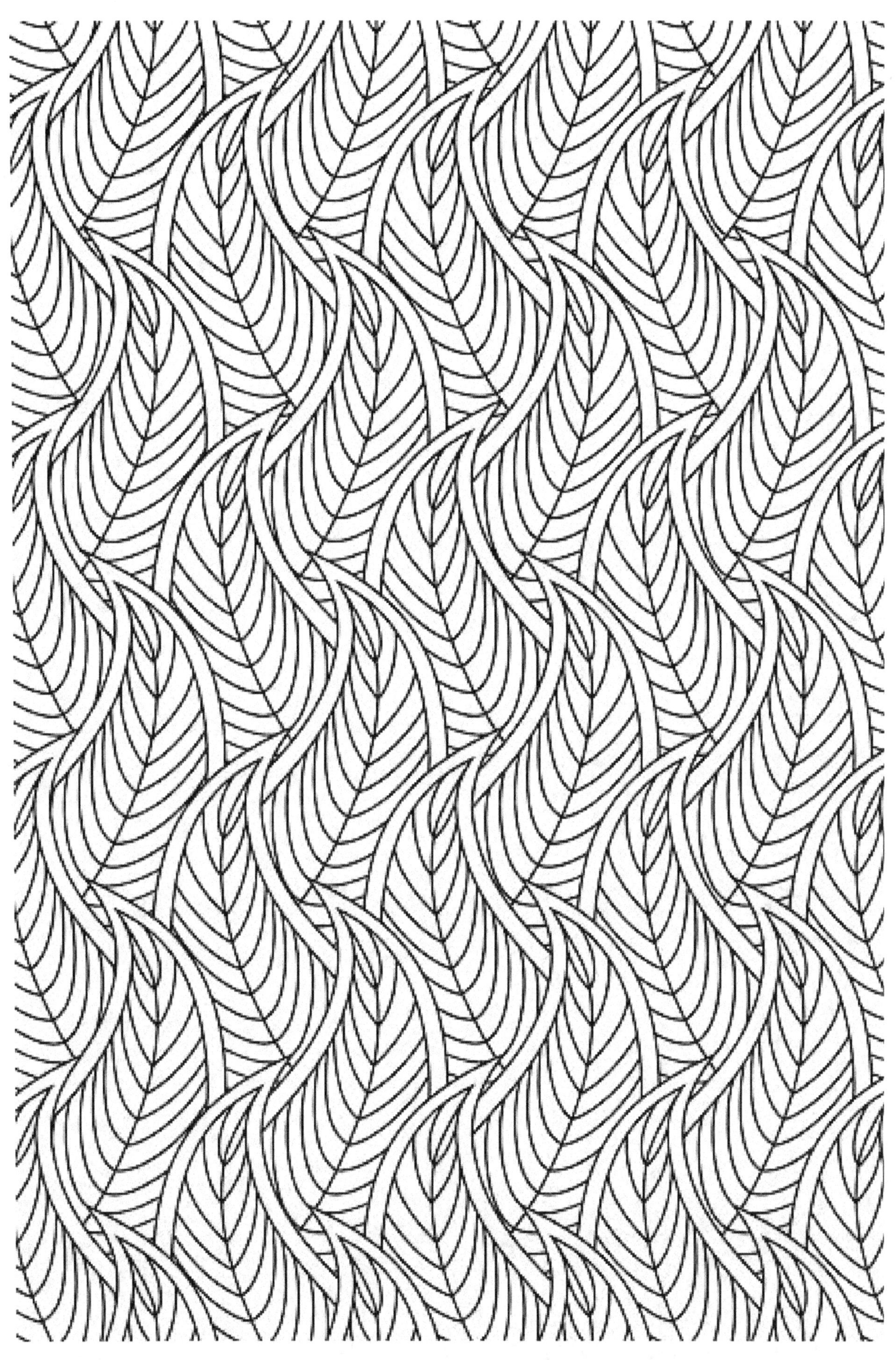

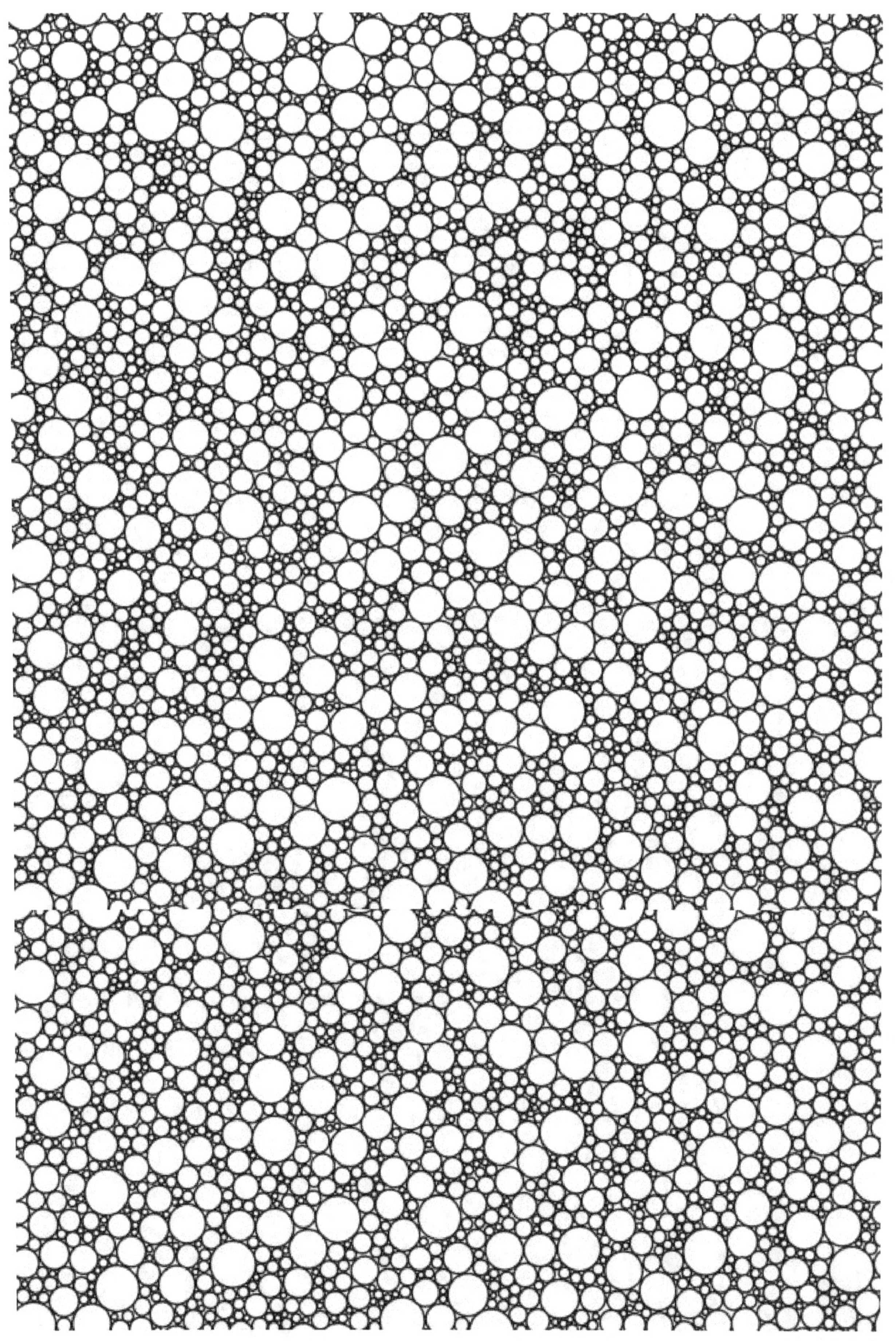

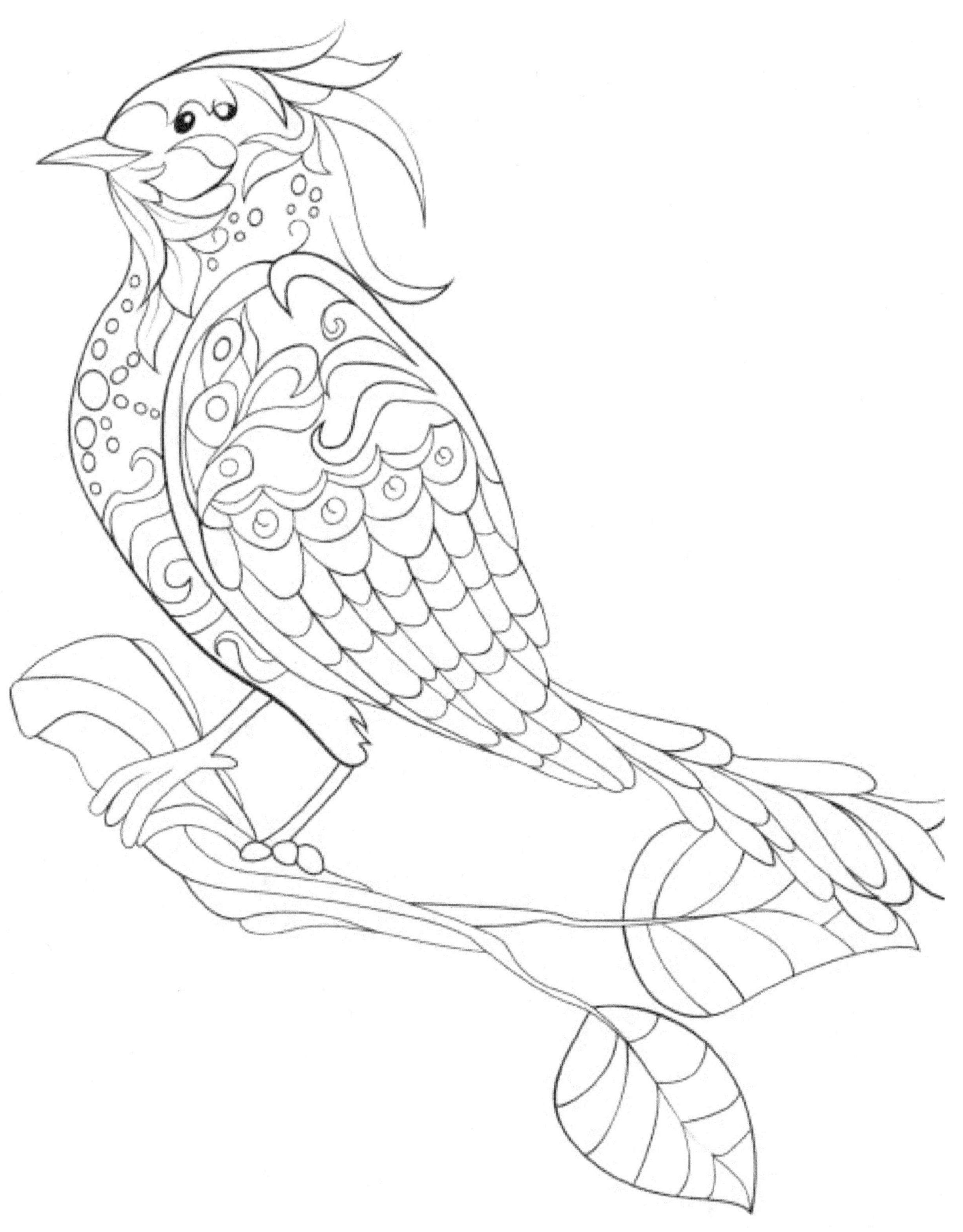

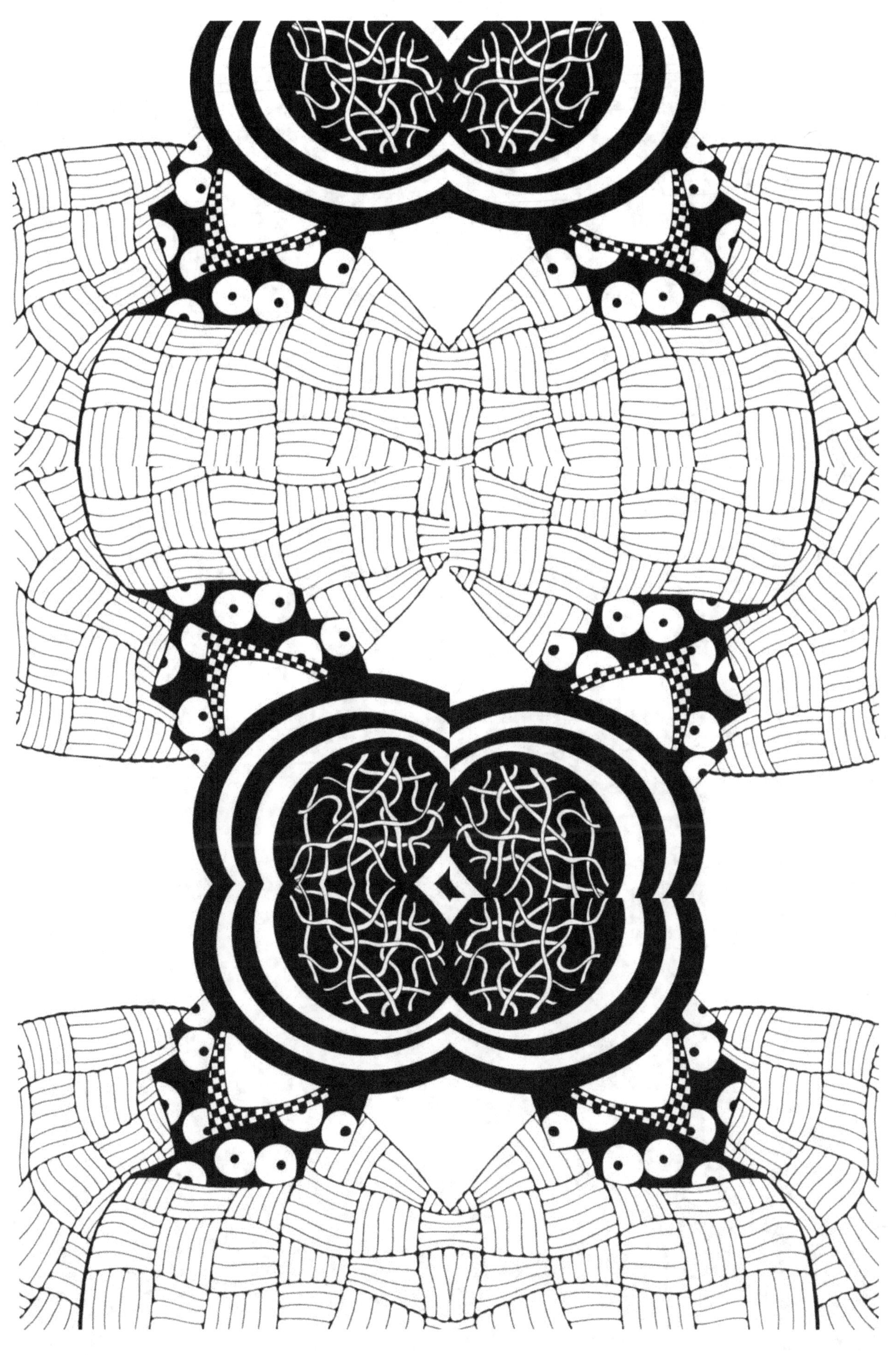

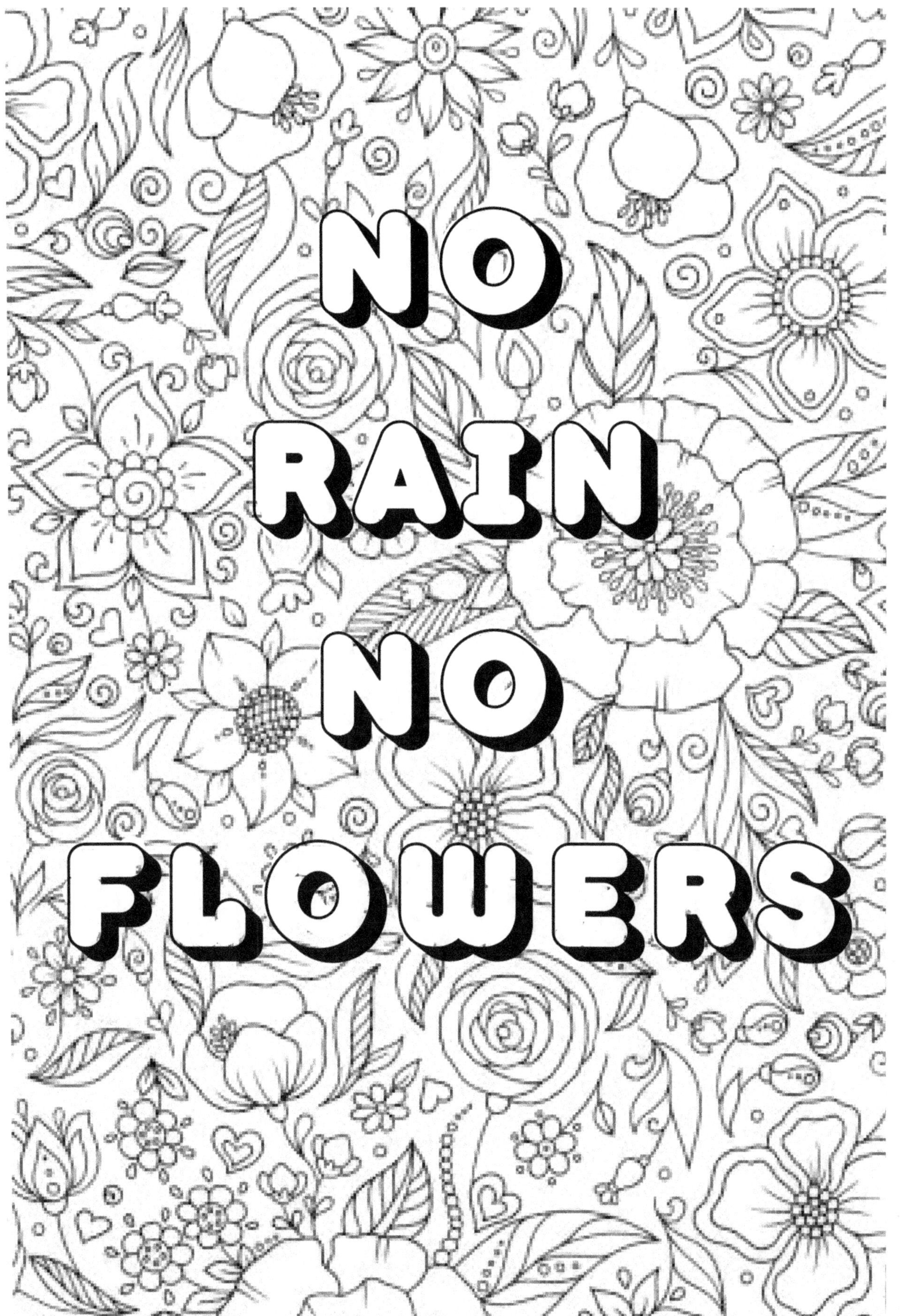

NO
RAIN
NO
FLOWERS

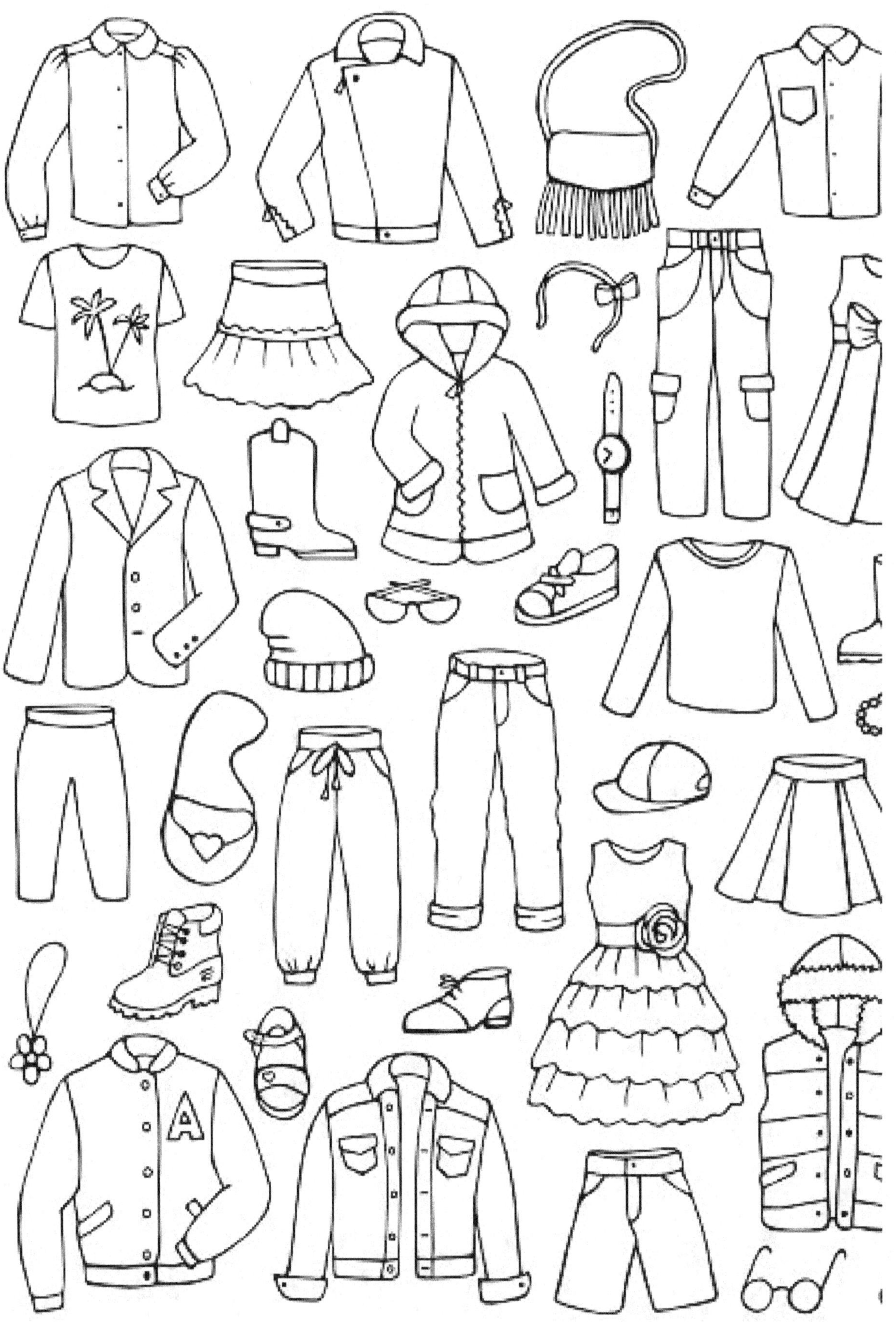

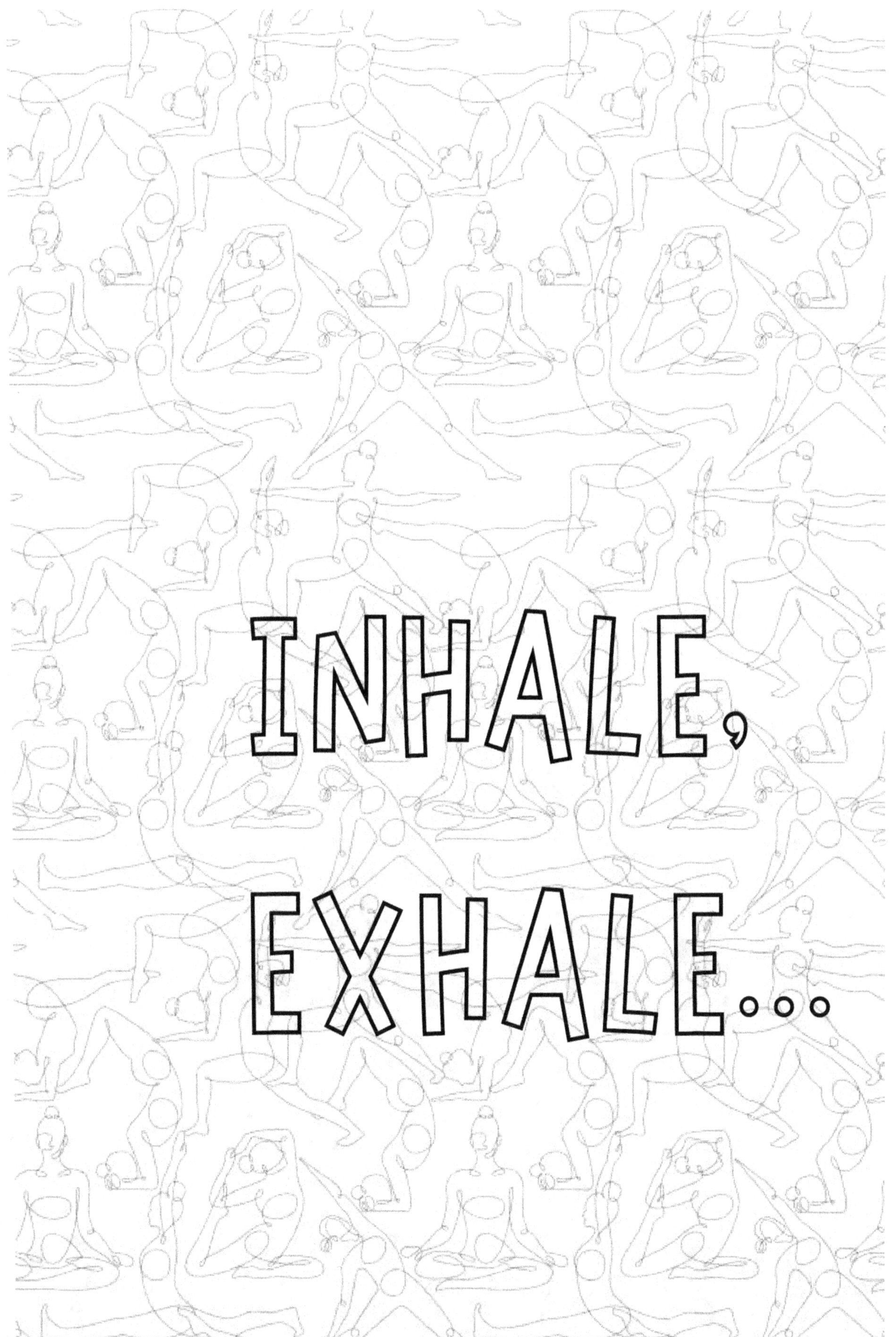
INHALE,
EXHALE...

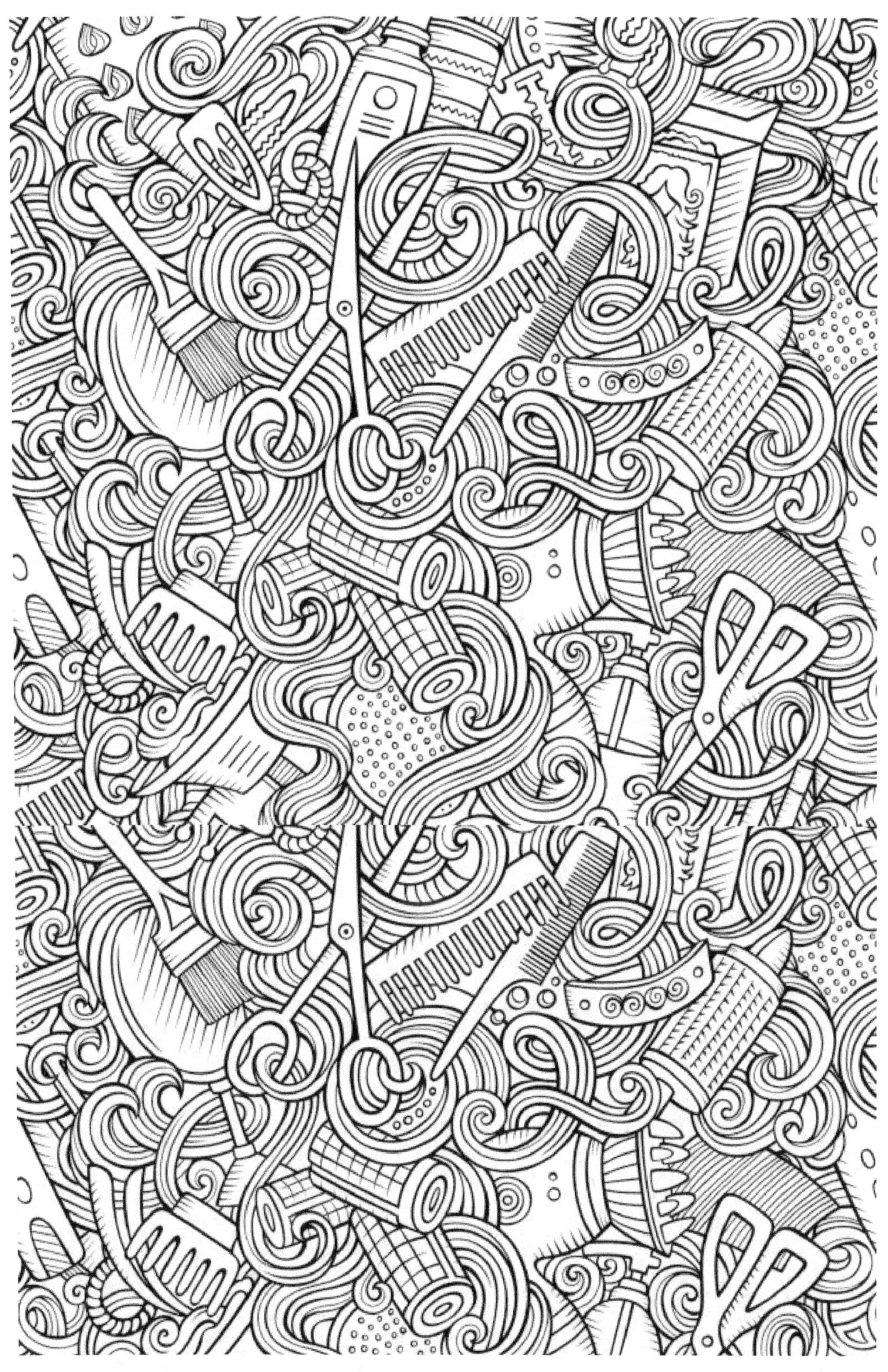

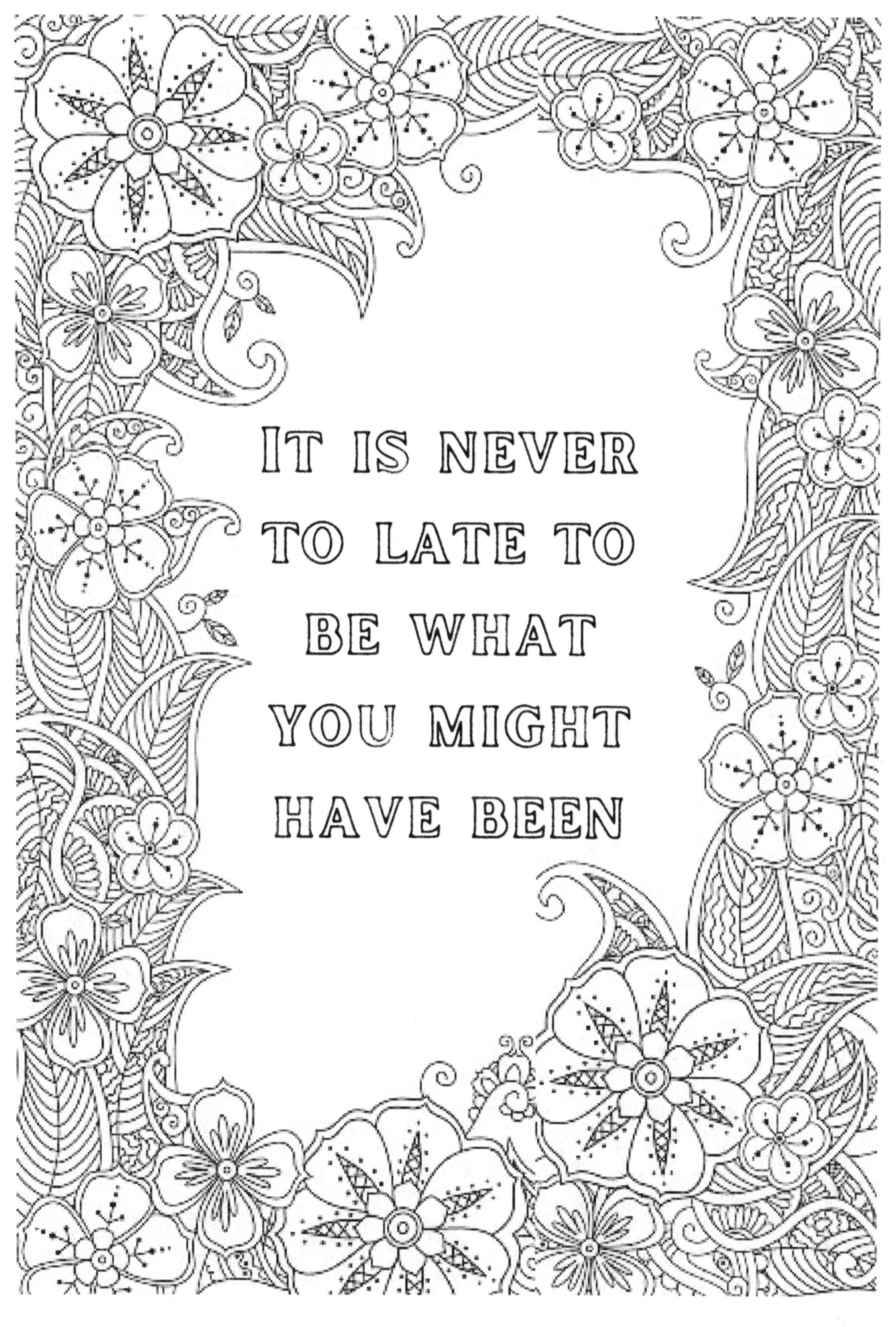

It is never
to late to
be what
you might
have been

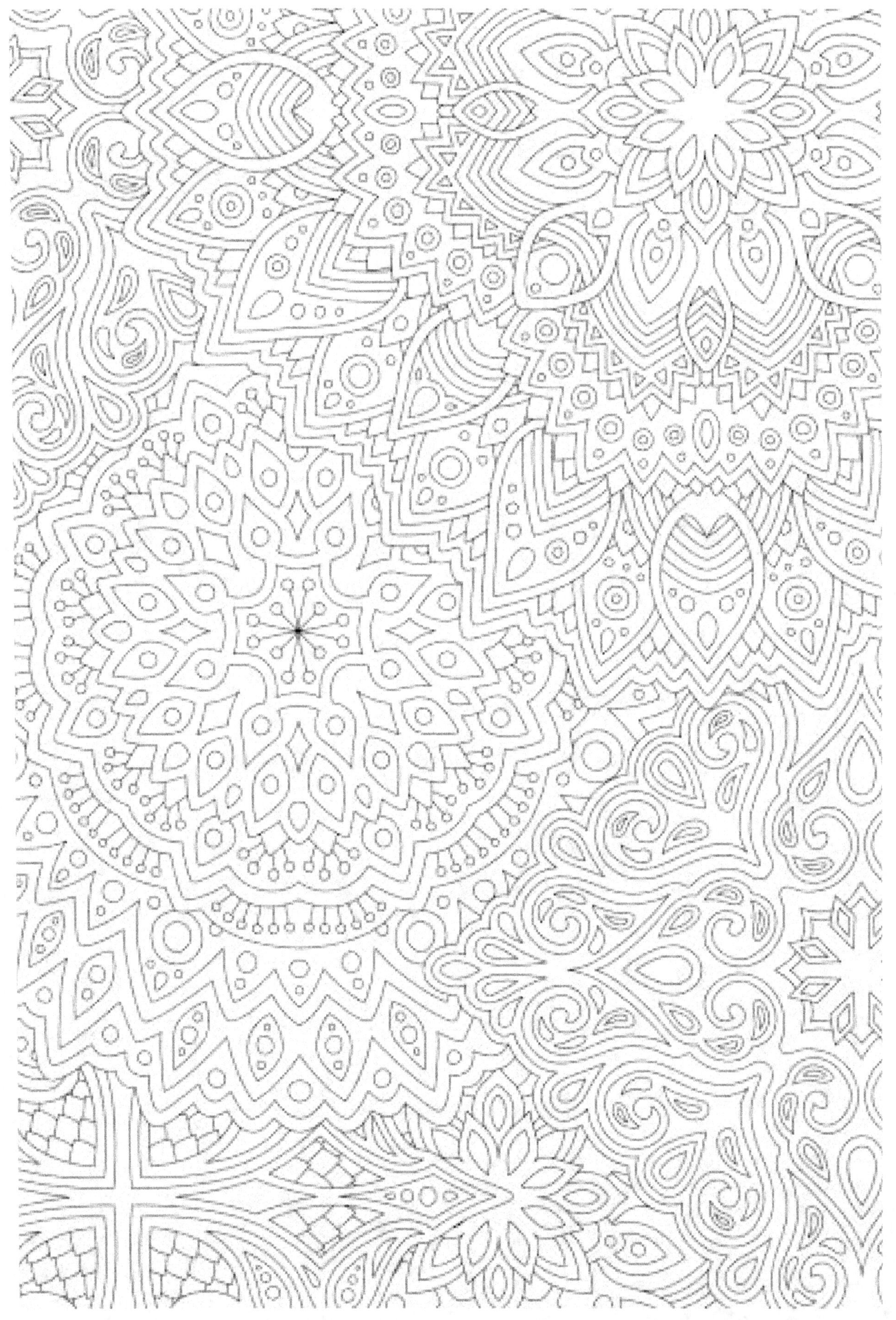

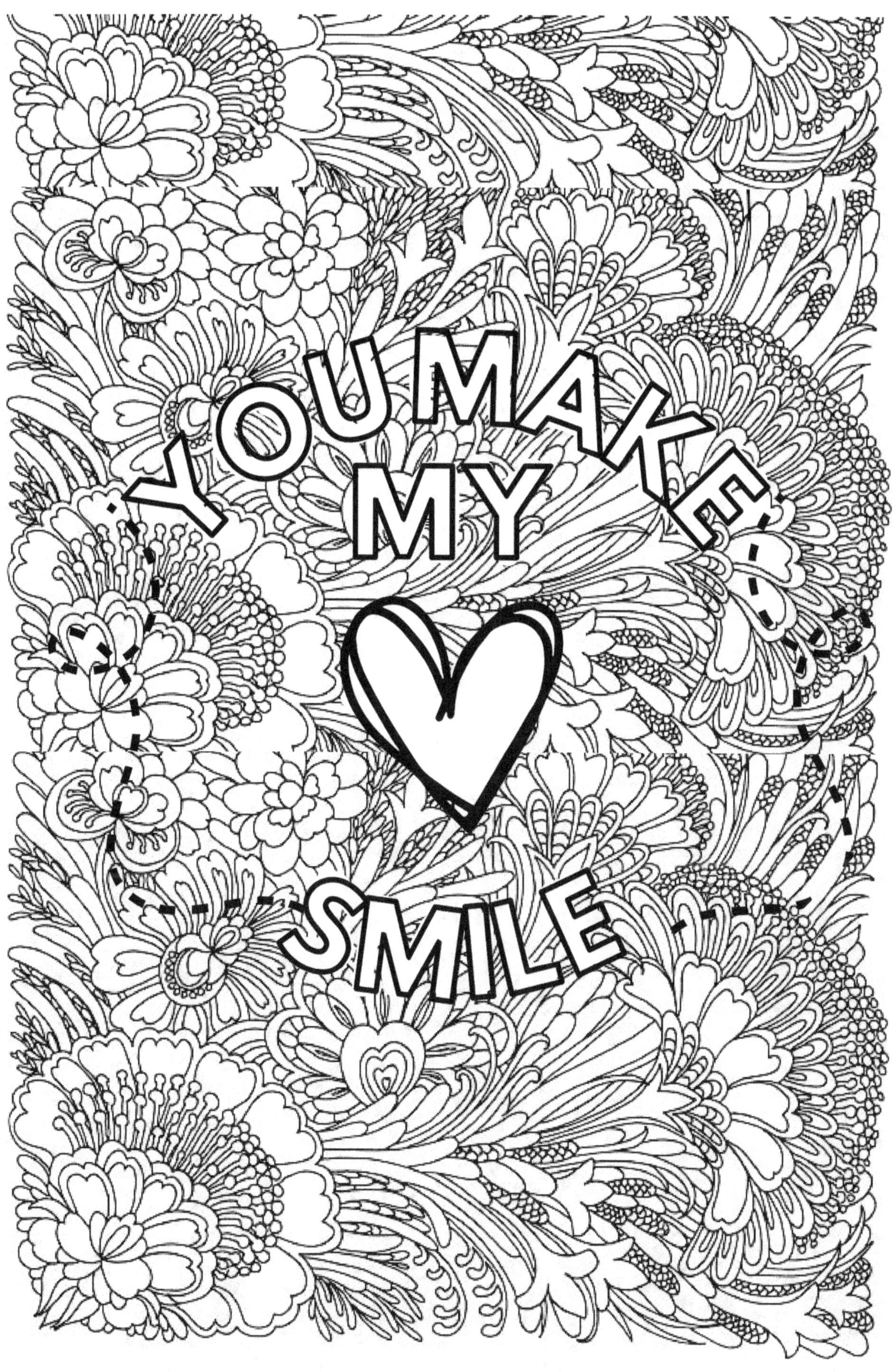

YOU MAKE MY
SMILE

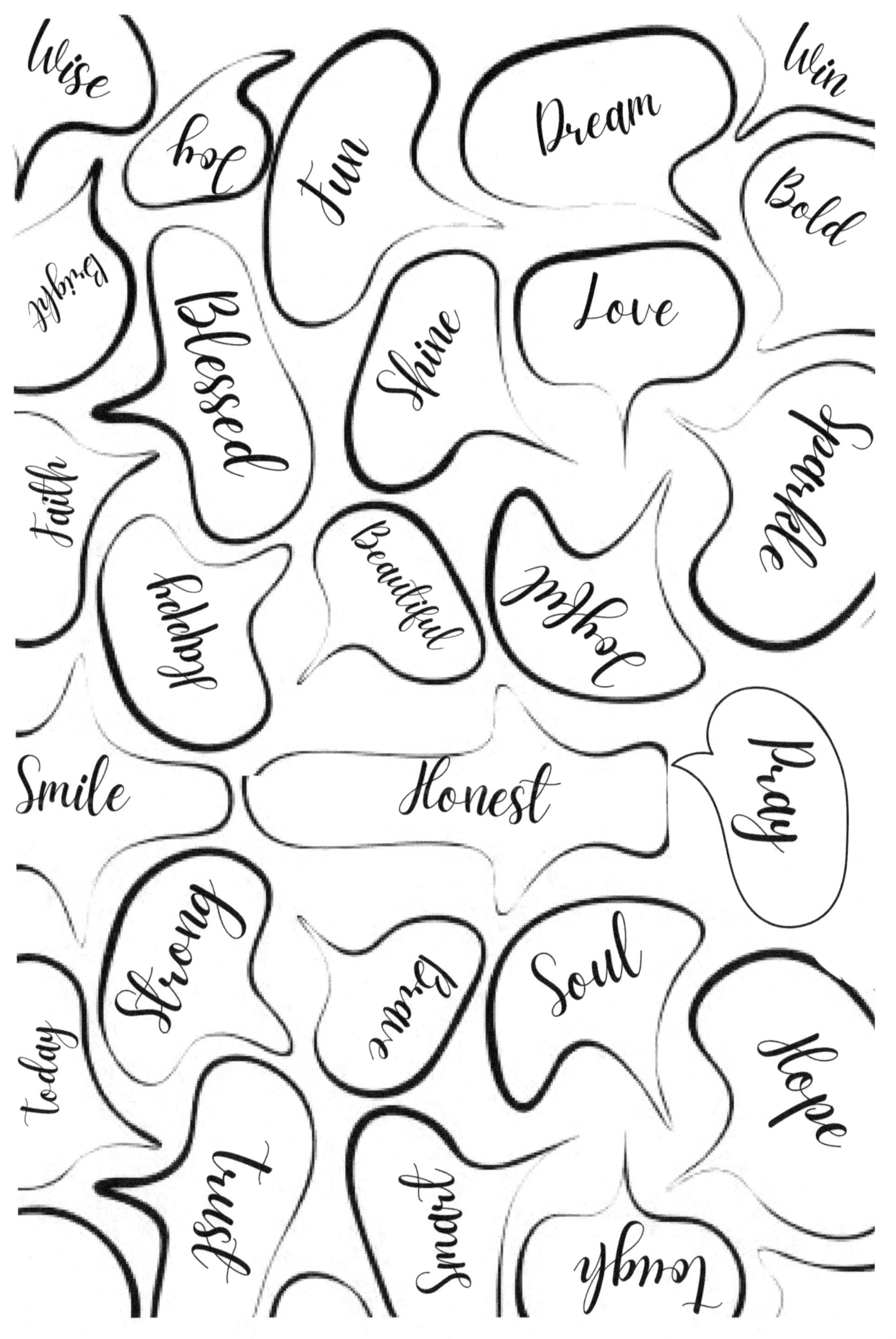

Wise
Joy
Fun
Dream
Win
Bold
Bright
Blessed
Shine
Love
Faith
Sparkle
Happy
Beautiful
Joyful
Smile
Honest
Pray
Strong
Brave
Soul
today
Hope
trust
Smart
Tough

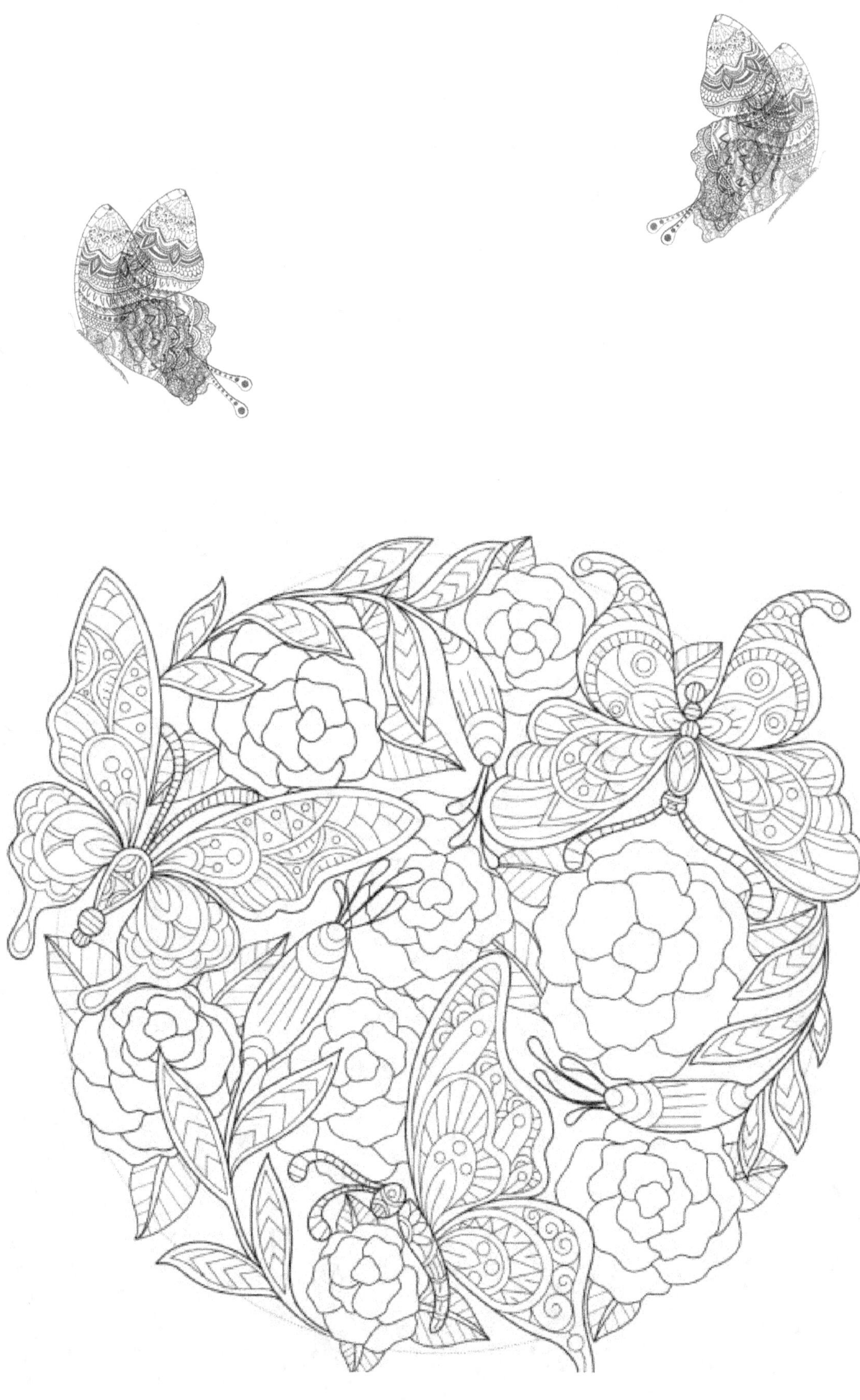

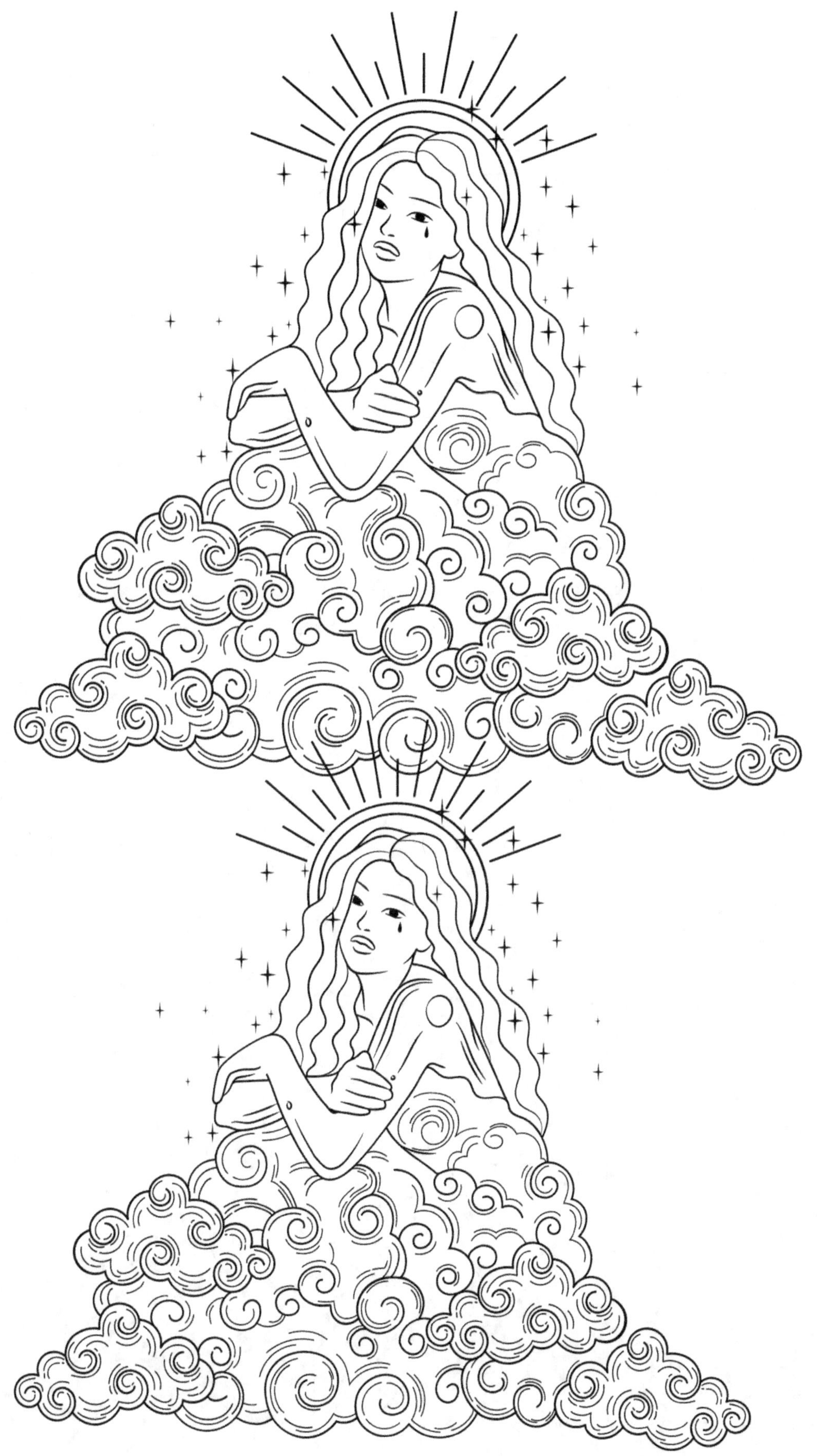

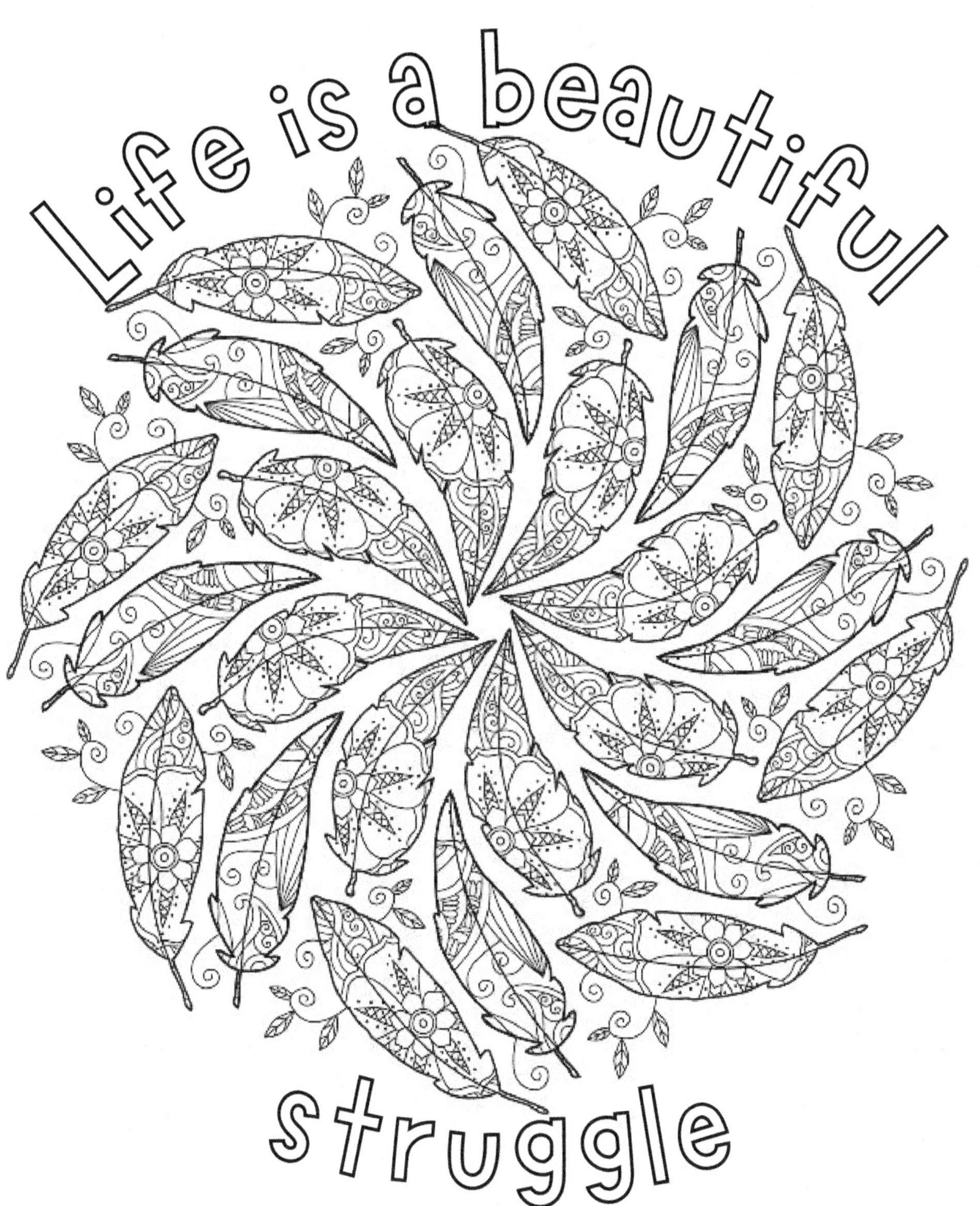
Life is a beautiful
struggle

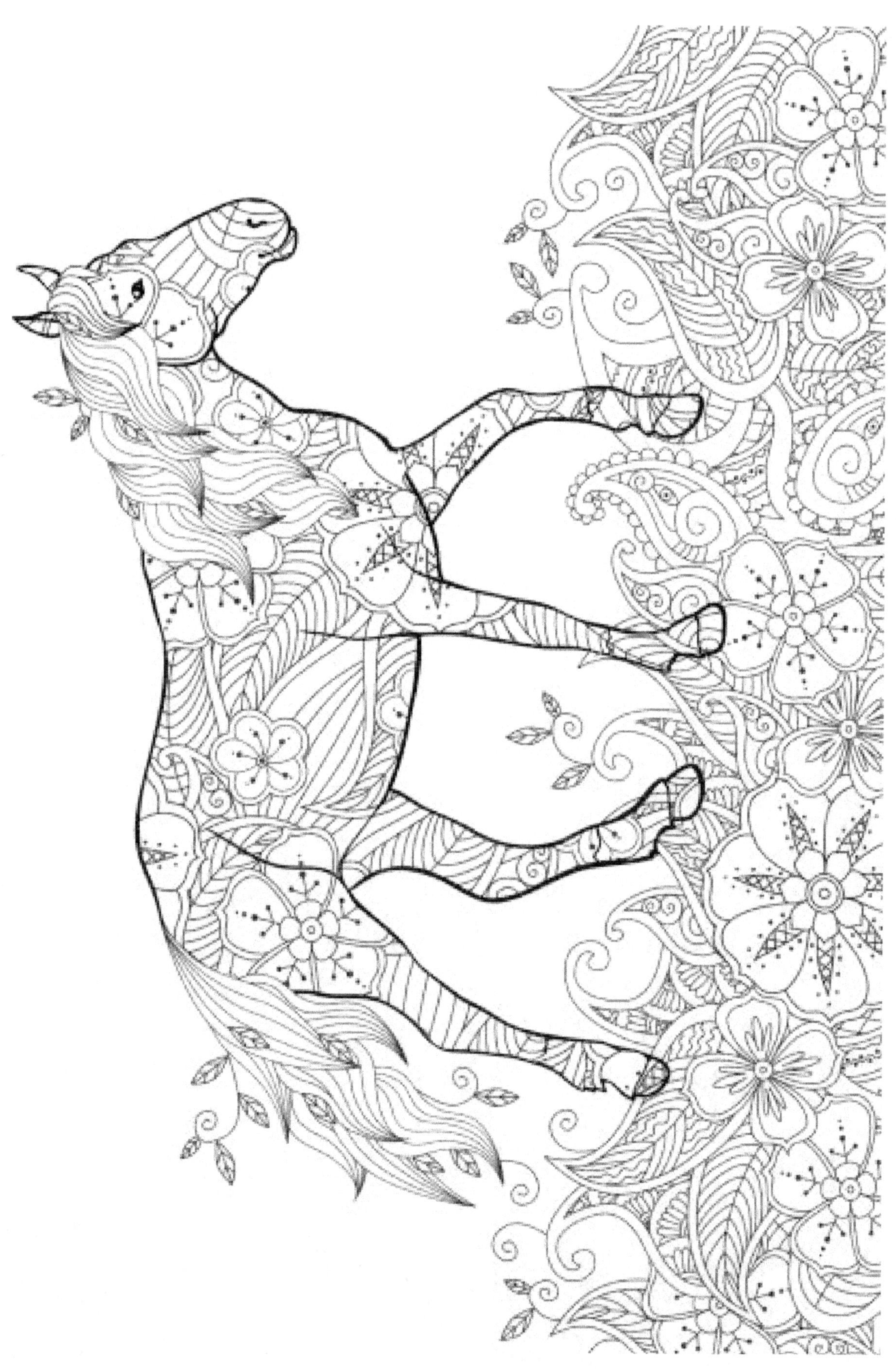

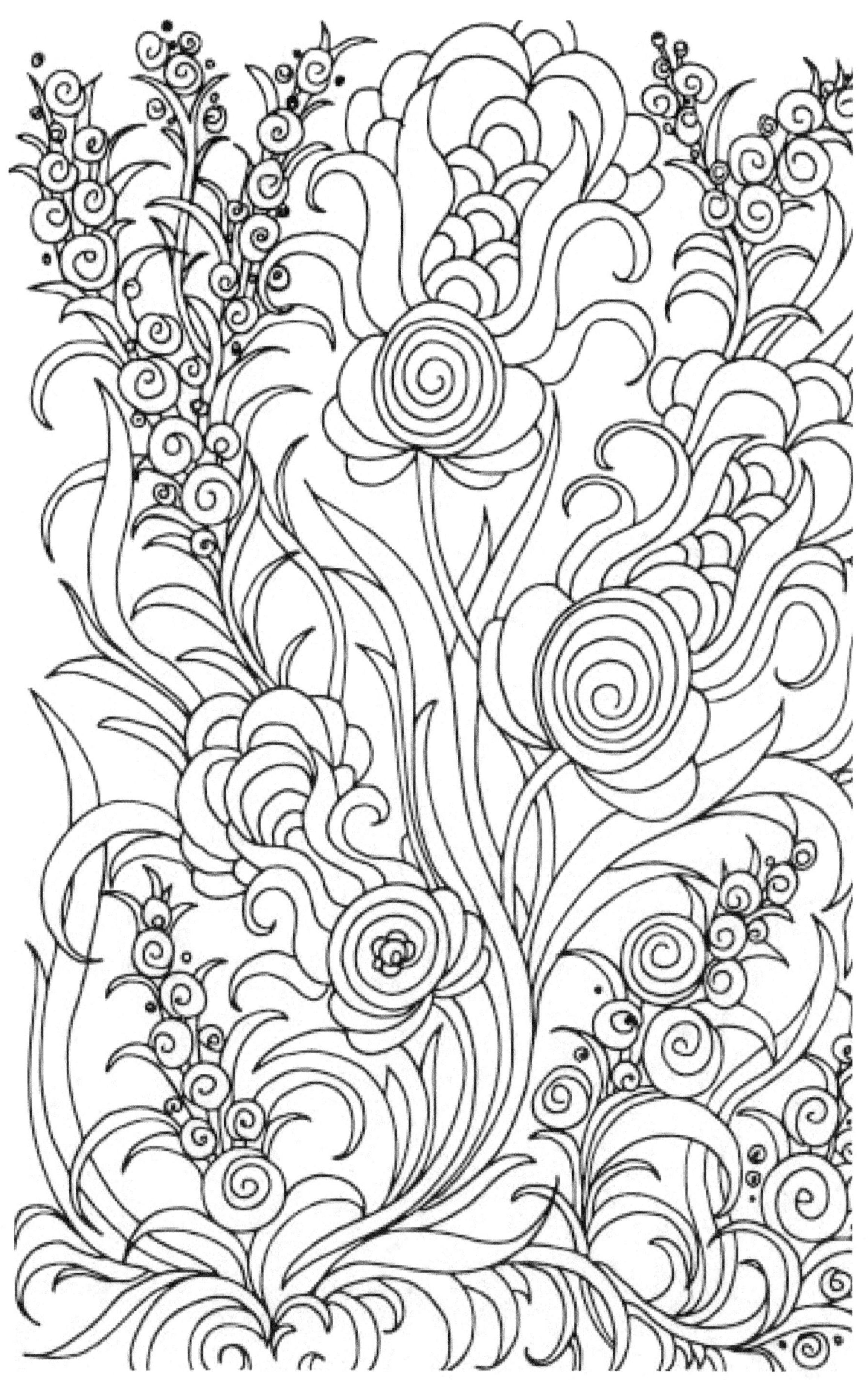

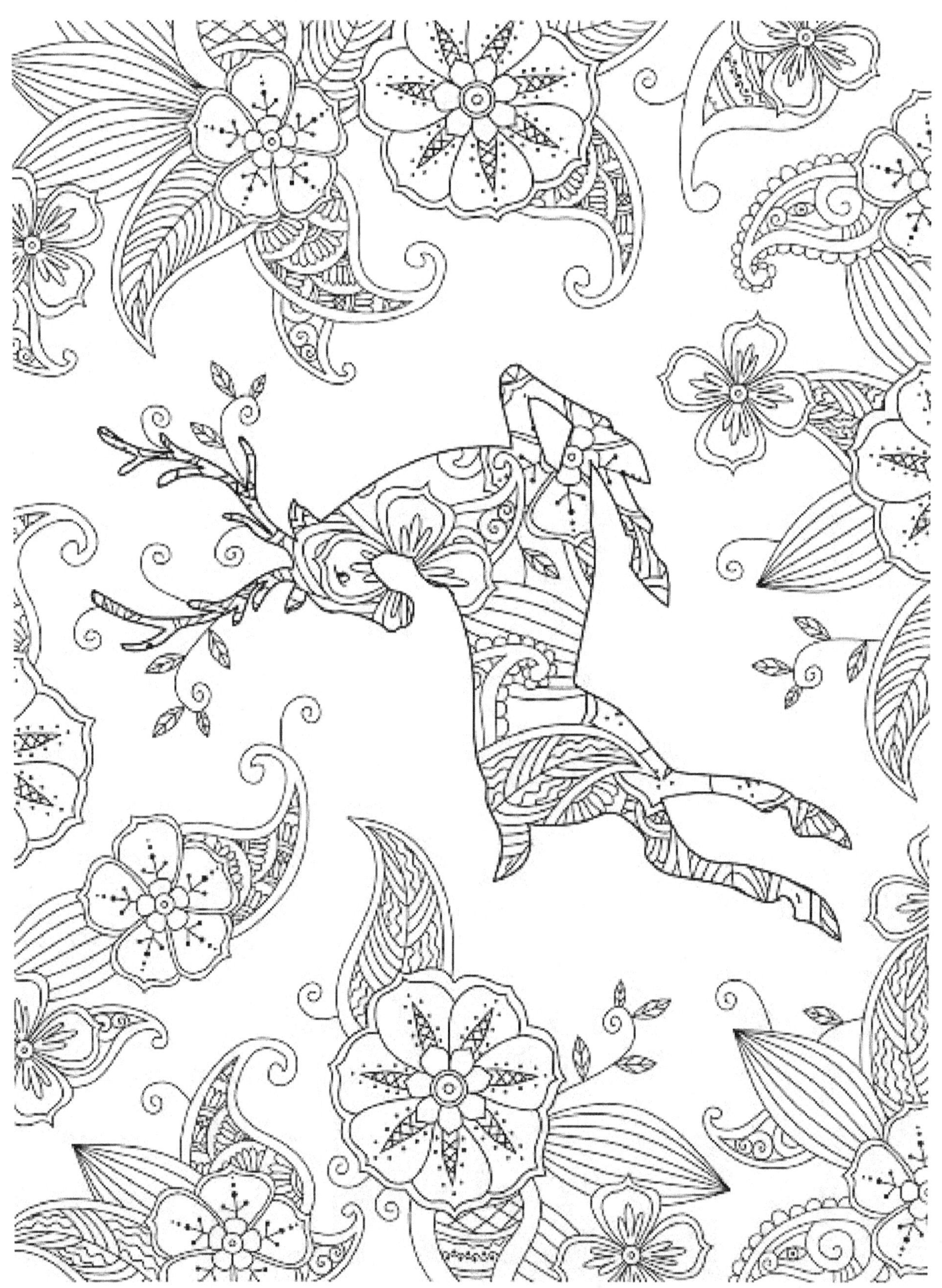

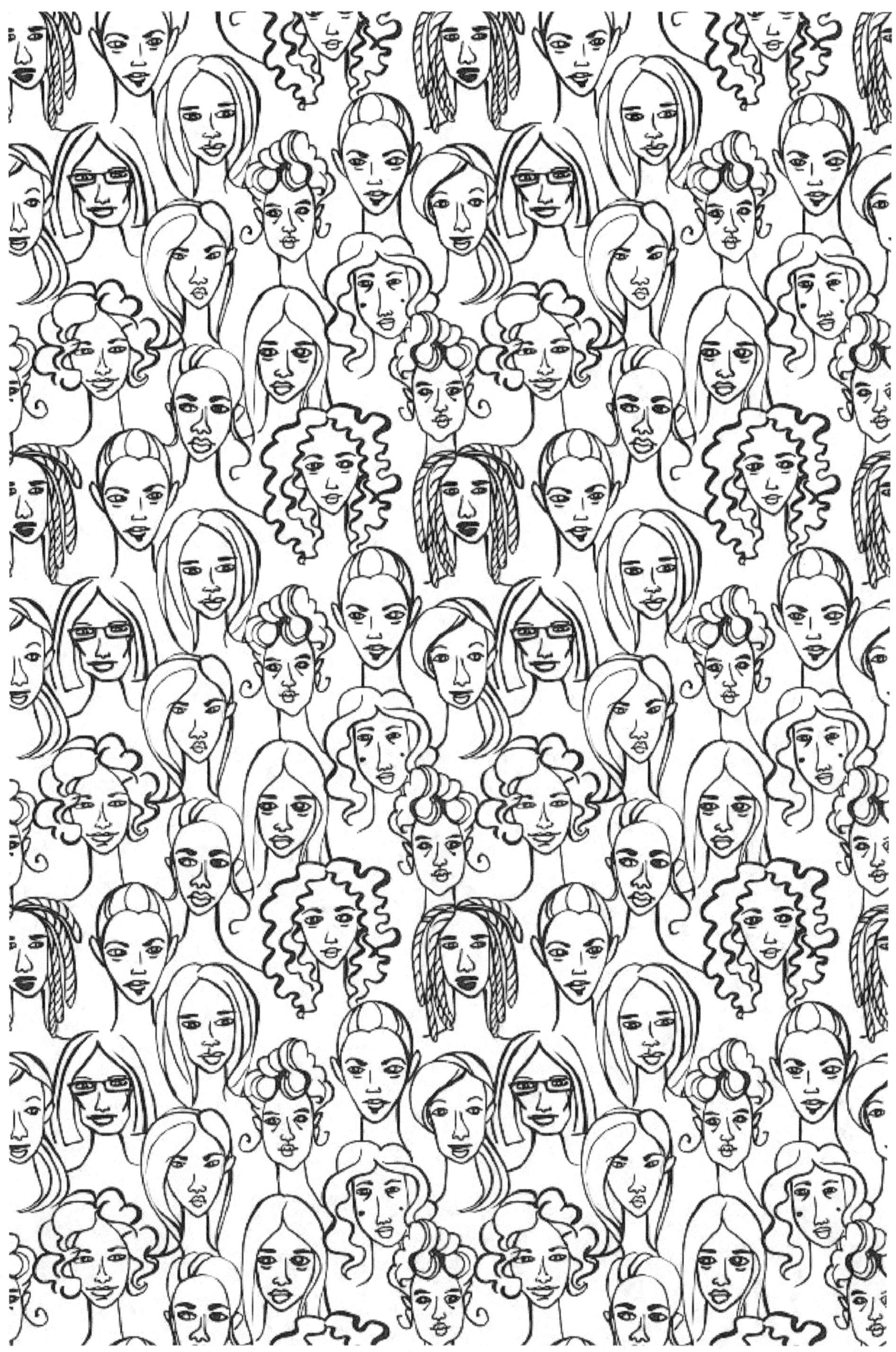

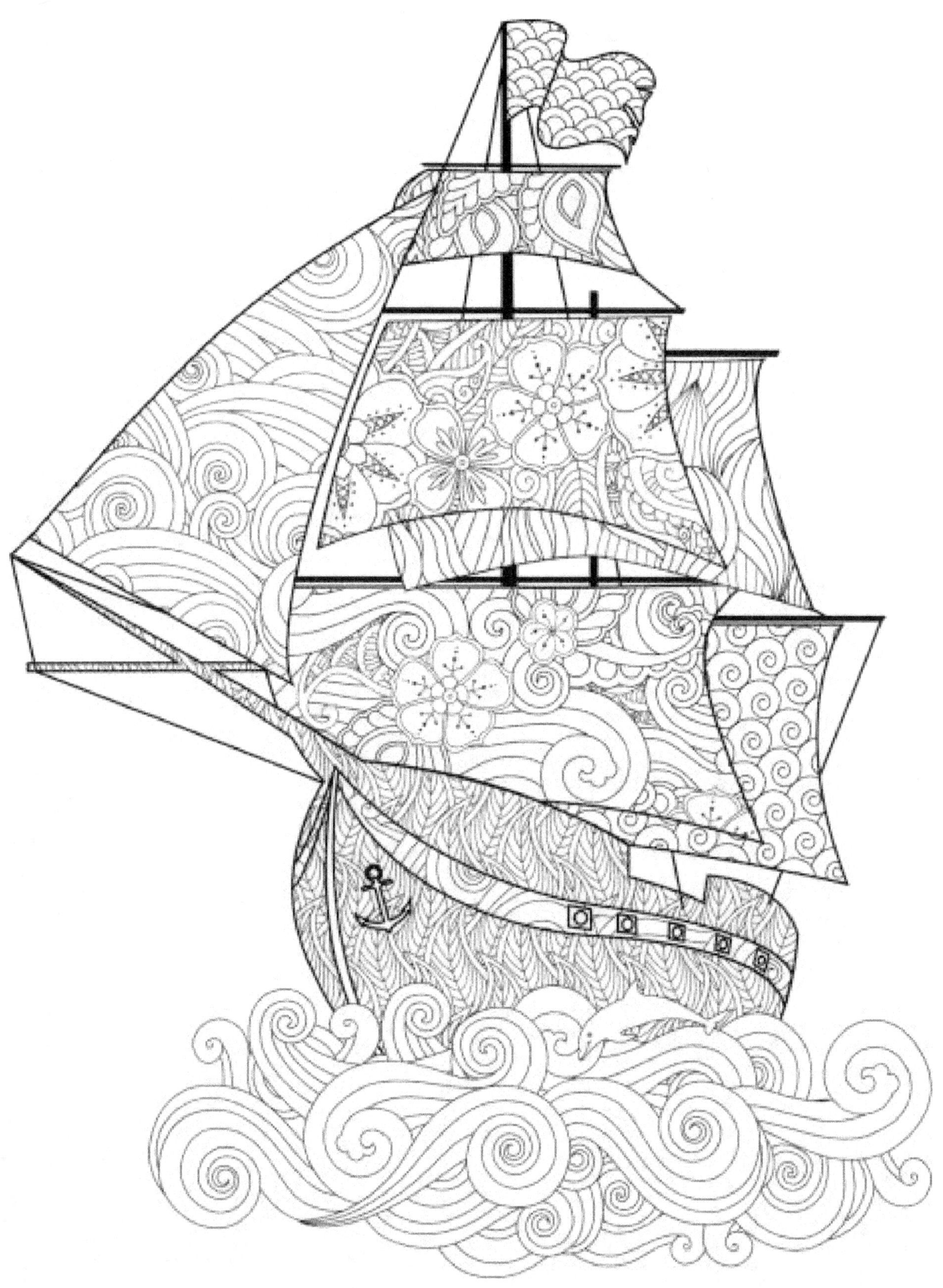

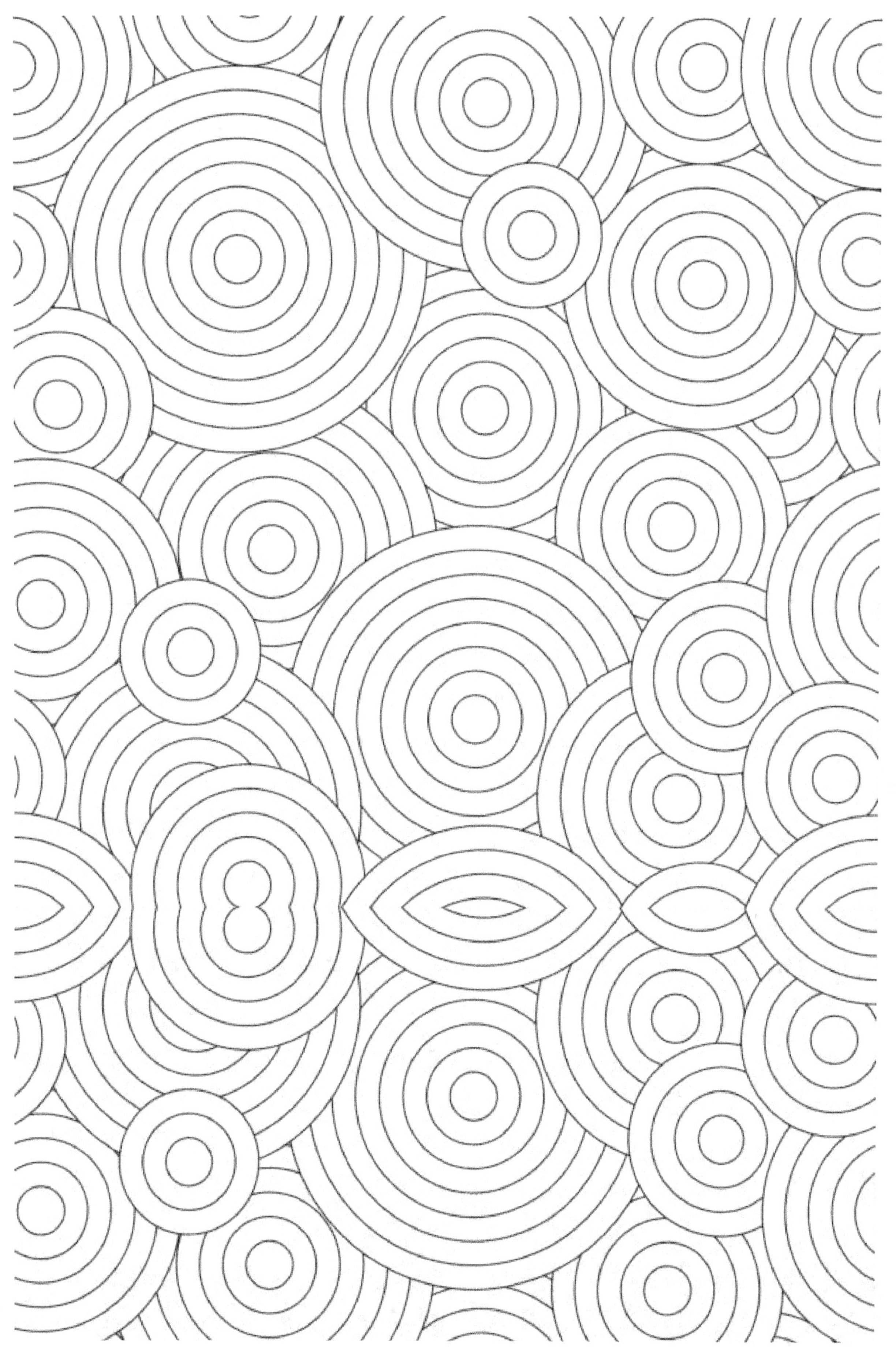

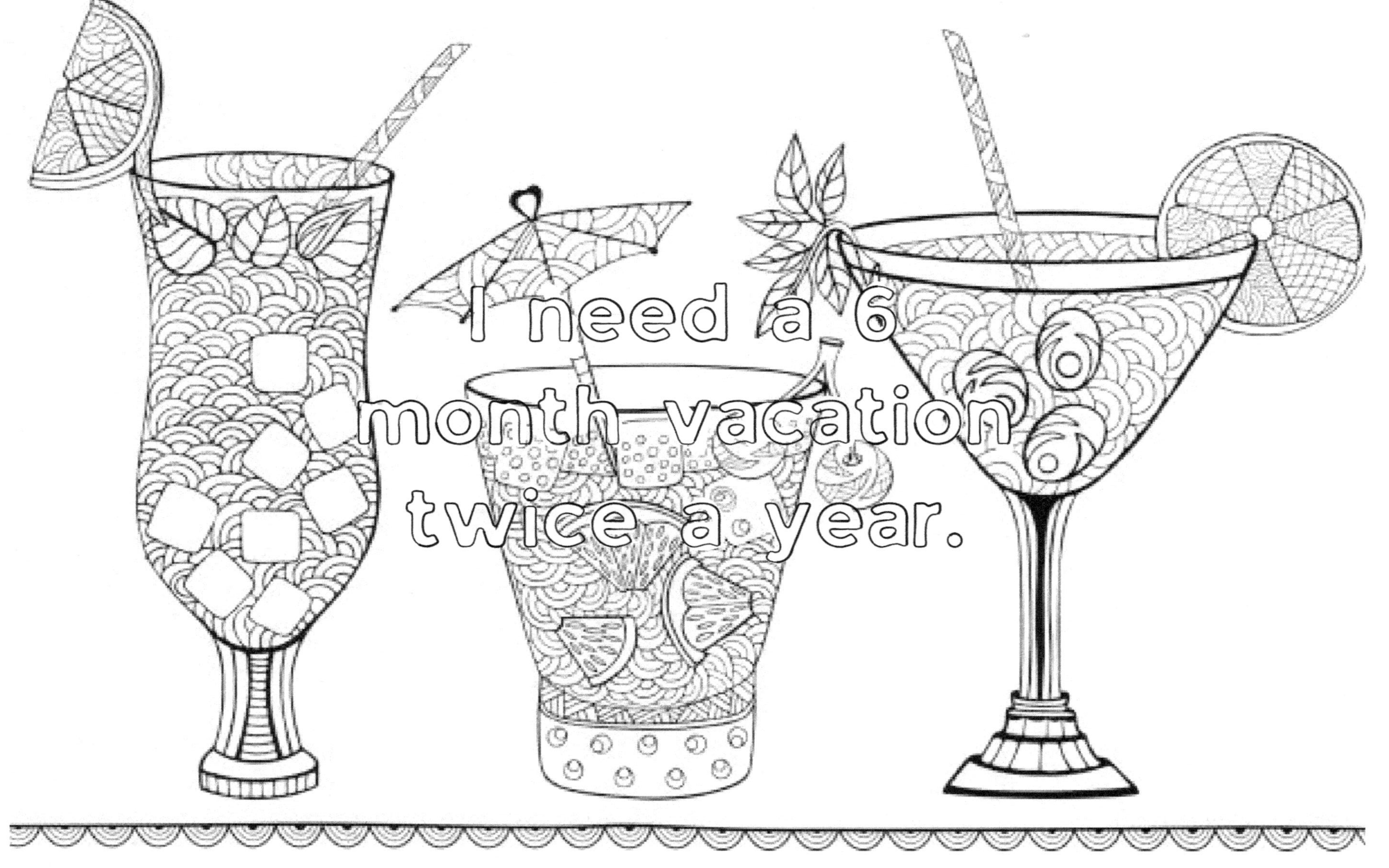

I need a 6
month vacation
twice a year.

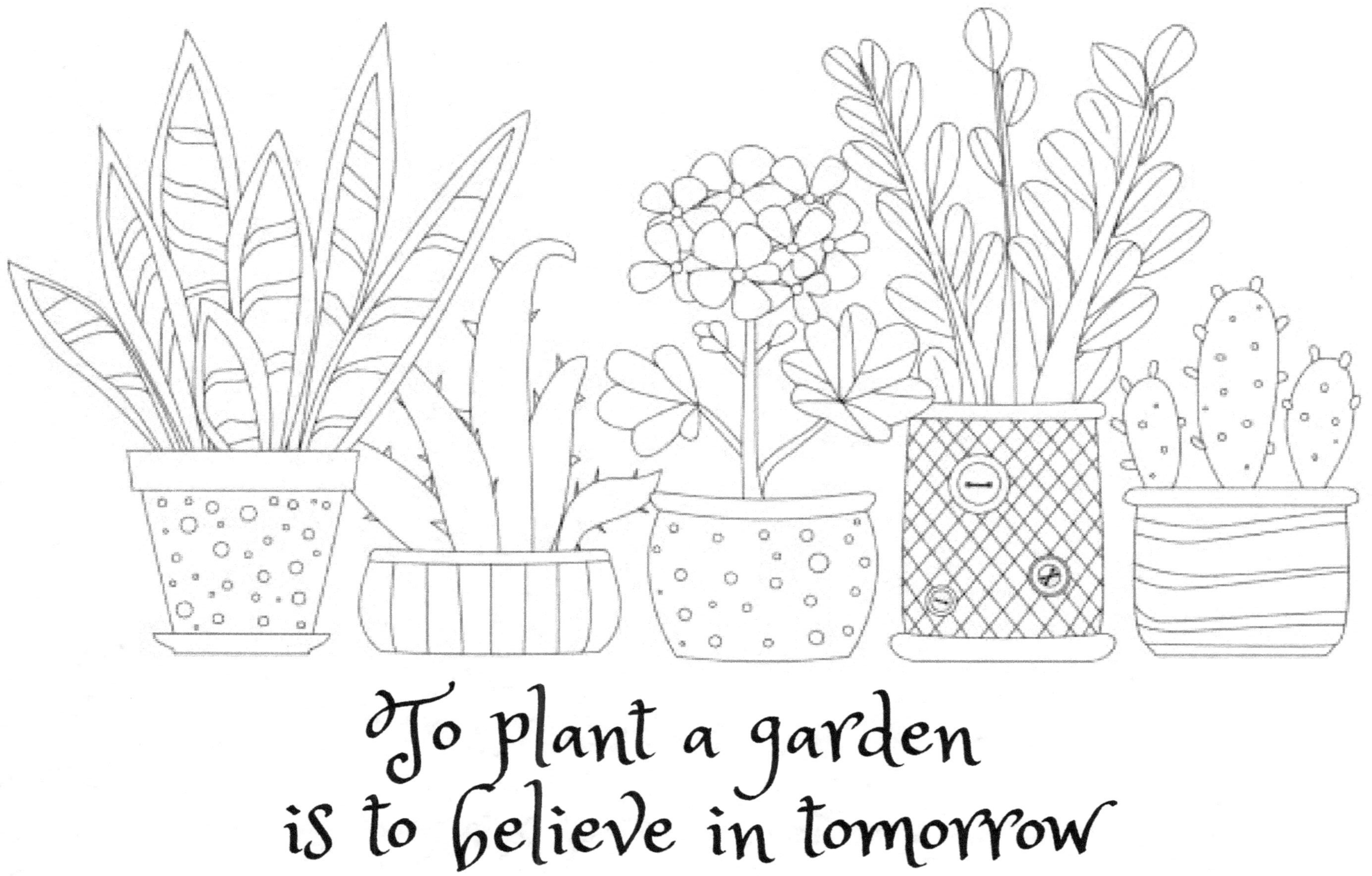

To plant a garden
is to believe in tomorrow

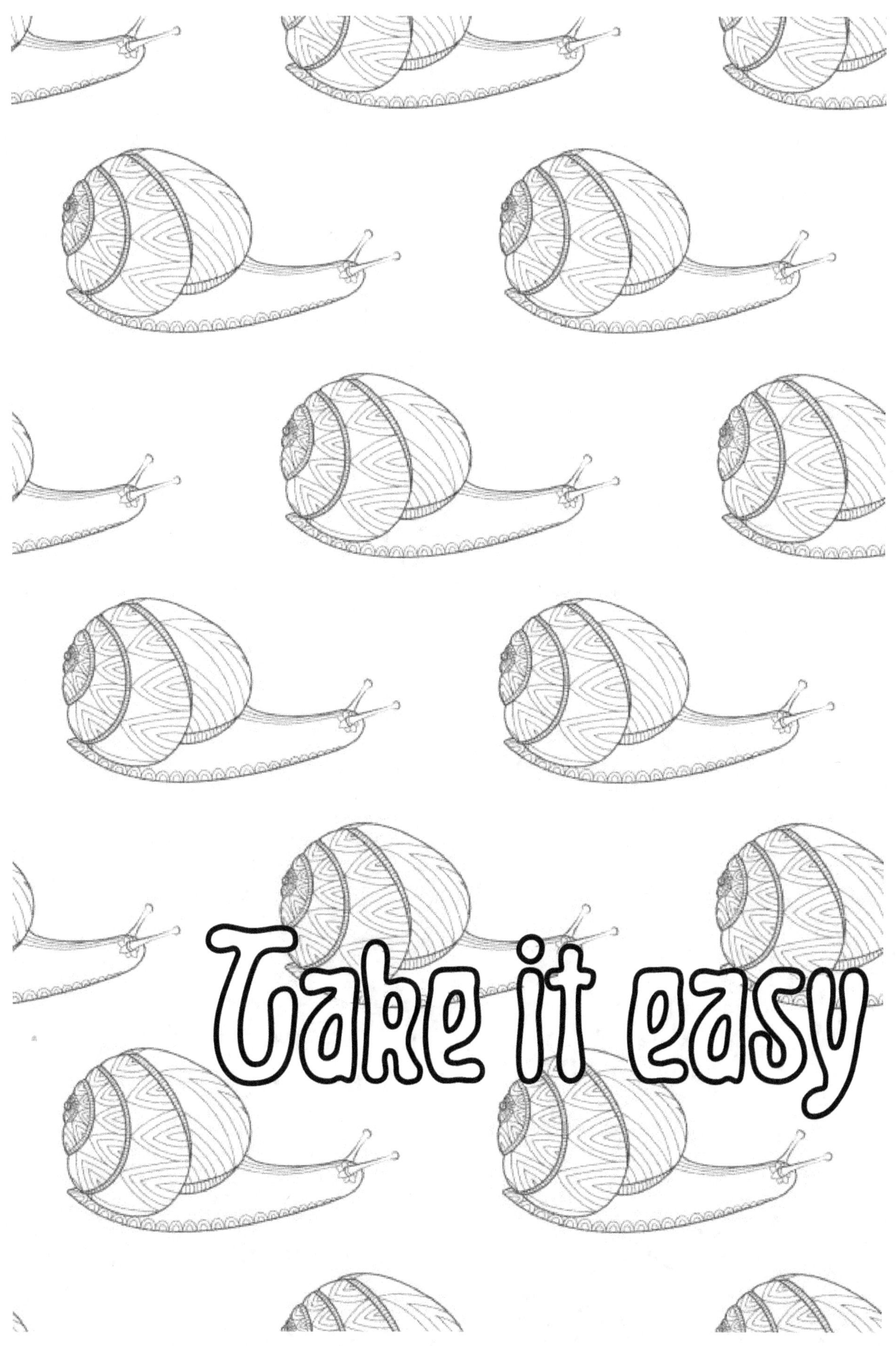
Take it easy

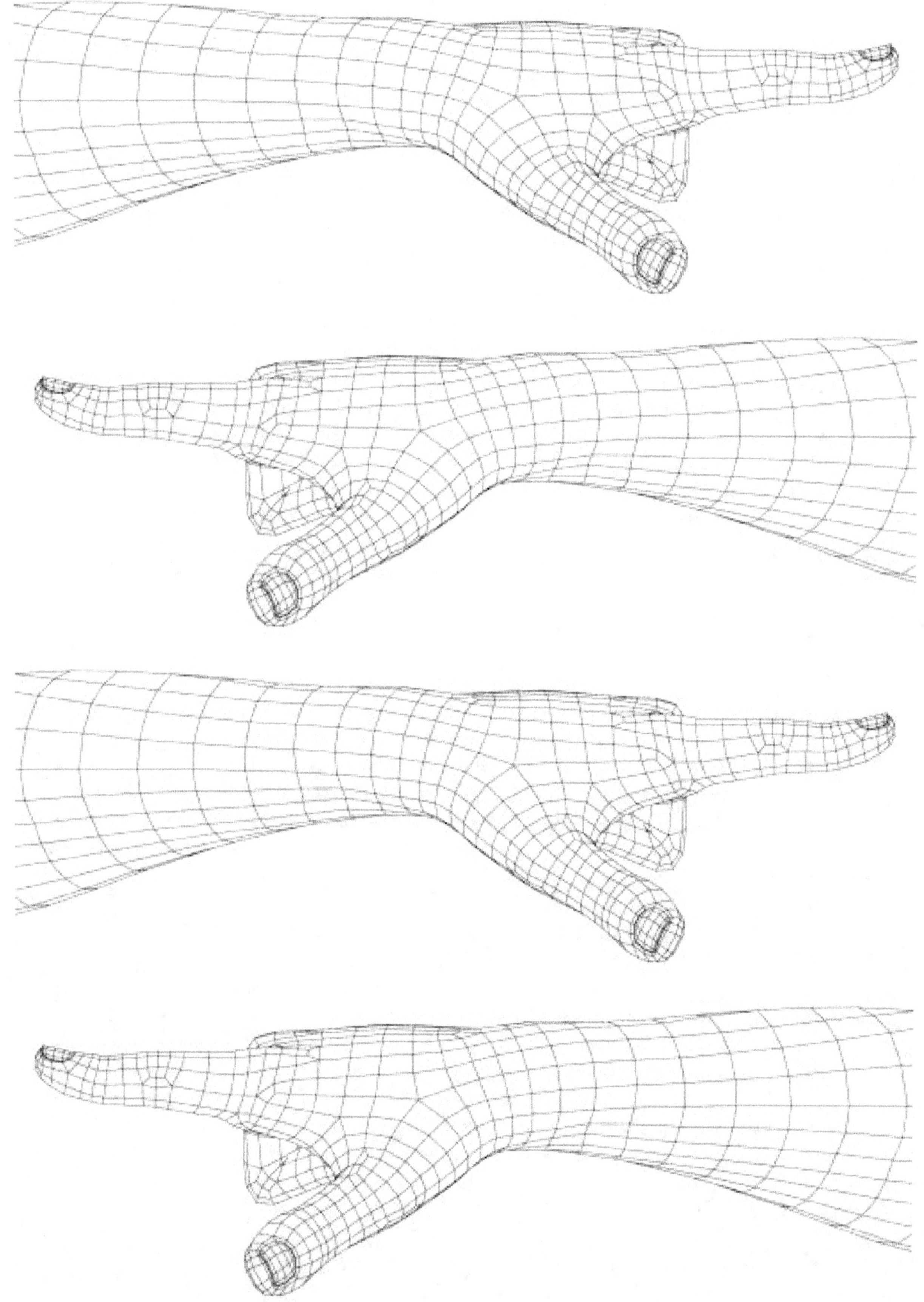

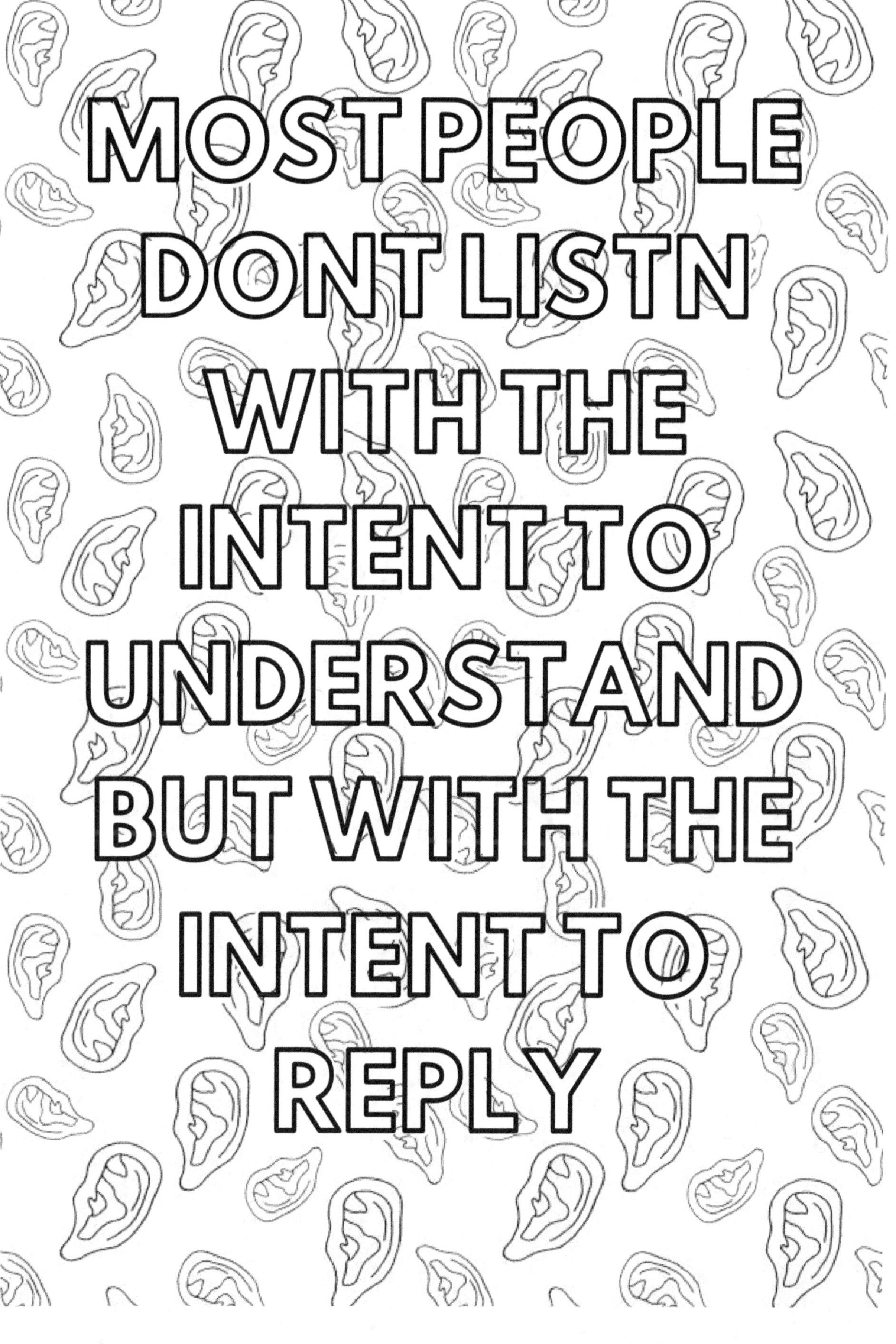

MOST PEOPLE
DONT LISTN
WITH THE
INTENT TO
UNDERSTAND
BUT WITH THE
INTENT TO
REPLY

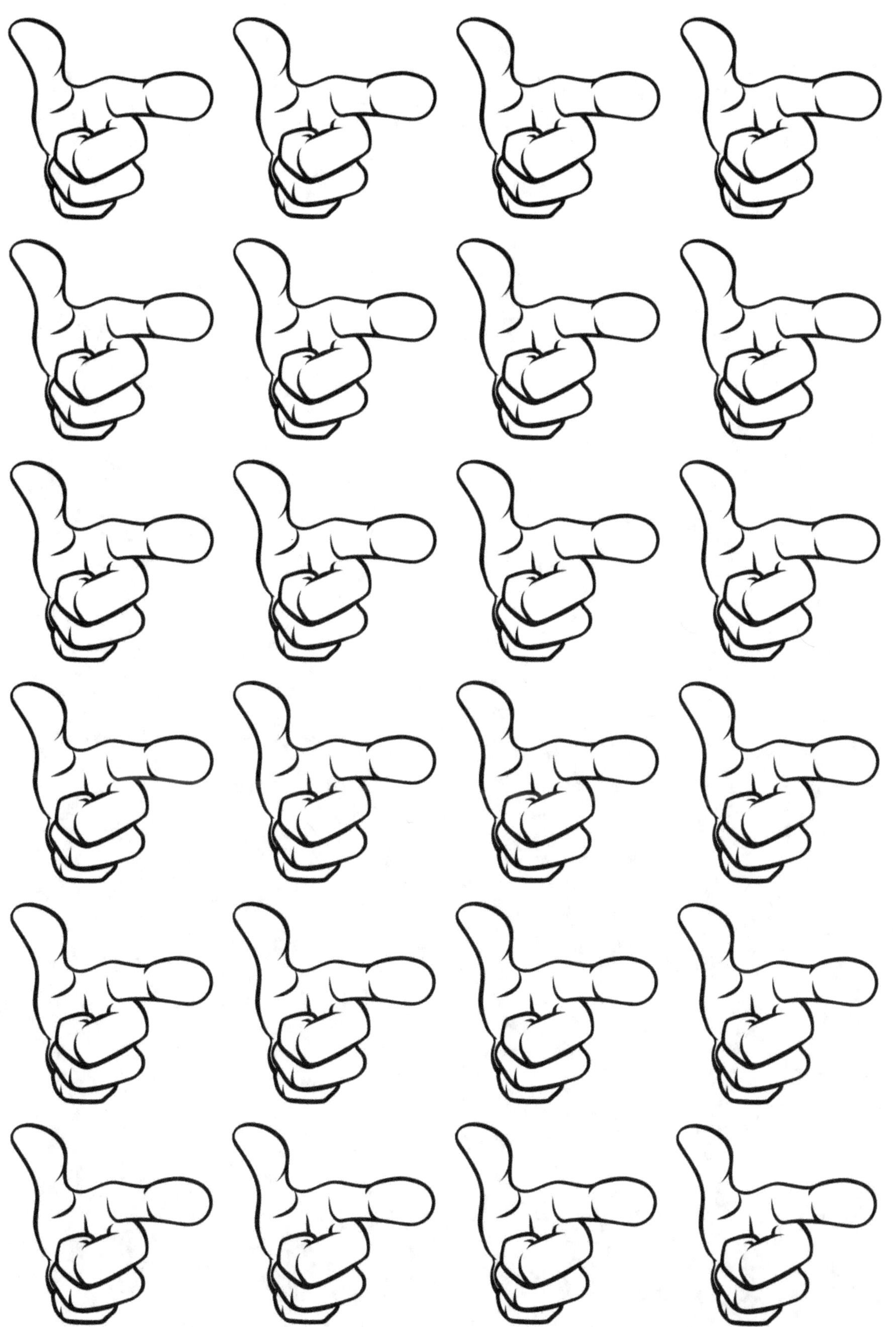

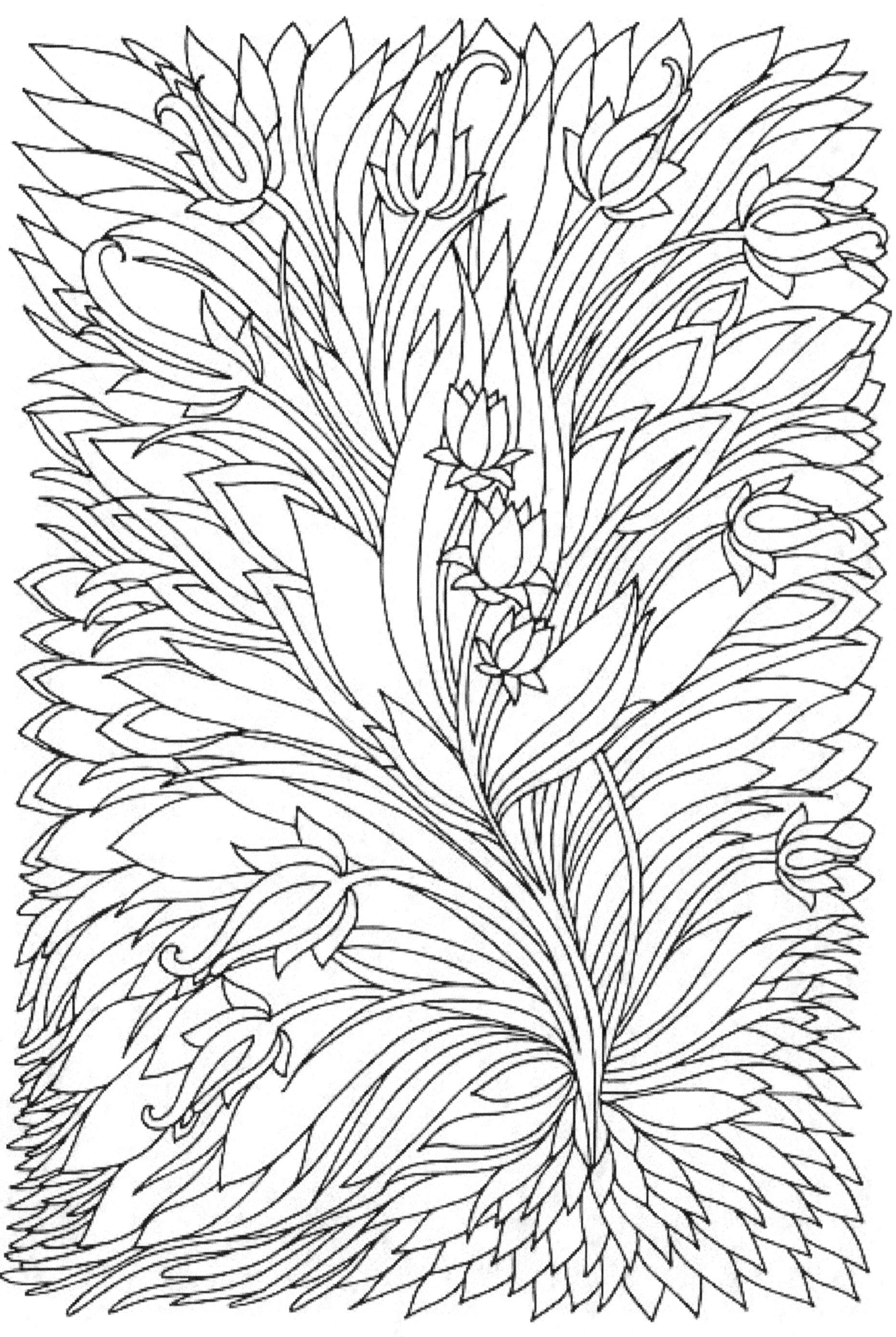

www.ingramcontent.com/pod-product-compliance
Lightning Source LLC
Chambersburg PA
CBHW081354160726
48000CB00010B/3339